Challenge

Level 3

Workbook

A Division of The McGraw·Hill Companies

Columbus, Ohio

www.sra4kids.com

SRA/McGraw-Hill

*A Division of The **McGraw·Hill** Companies*

Copyright © 2002 by SRA/McGraw-Hill.

Send all inquiries to:
SRA/McGraw-Hill
4400 Easton Commons
Columbus, OH 43219

Printed in the United States of America.

ISBN 0-07-572045-0

6 7 8 9 10 11 12 QPD 09

Table of Contents

Unit 3 Imagination

Unit 4 Money

UNIT I Friendship • **Lesson I** *Gloria Who Might Be My Best Friend*

▶ The /a/ Sound

 Consonant Substitution Strategy Make two new words by changing the underlined letter or letters in each word. Then write a sentence using one of the new words.

SPELLING

1. <u>p</u>ath _____

_____

2. <u>l</u>amp _____

_____

3. <u>pl</u>an<u>t</u> _____

_____

 Visualization Strategy Circle the correct spelling for each word. Then write it on the line.

1. crach   crash   crashe _____

2. hatbocks hatboxe hatbox _____

3. stampe   stamp   stanp   _____

4. black   blach   blac   _____

5. theat   thet   that   _____

▶Vocabulary Strategies

▶Fill in the blank with a word from the box that makes sense in each sentence.

suspect	recent	angle	custom	imitate	finely

1. The two lines met in a 90-degree _____.

2. This week's _____ events caused us to act quickly.

3. Can you _____ a quacking duck?

4. _____ chop the onion into tiny pieces.

5. Do you _____ your wallet was stolen?

6. The Chinese have a _____ of celebrating the New Year with fancy parades.

VOCABULARY

▶Use the following words in a sentence to show their meaning.

1. thread _____

2. fence _____

Name _____ Date _____

▶ Nouns

Proper nouns refer to a particular person, place, or thing and are always capitalized. Common nouns name any of a group of persons, places, or things.

After each sentence with an underlined proper noun, write a common noun of the same kind, and vice-versa. For example, after *The Titanic sailed from England*, you would write *The ship*.

1. My <u>school</u> closed early for parent-teacher conferences.

_____

2. The <u>Hyatt Regency</u> is located at 6th and Elm.

_____

3. The <u>car</u> comes with a built-in CD player.

_____

4. The <u>Empire State Building</u> is in New York City.

_____

5. <u>Van Gogh</u> used bold colors in his paintings.

_____

6. Our <u>teacher</u> took education courses to learn to teach.

_____

Name _____ Date _____

▶ Cause and Effect

▶ **Draw a line to match each cause to the effect it would have.**

Cause	**Effect**
1. They had finished the mural.	Heidi took her watch to a jeweler to be fixed.
2. She had left it at her friend's house.	Jason and Carl loaded the crate in the truck.
3. It had stopped running.	Sue and Jim cleaned the brushes and put them away.
4. They had finished packing it.	The puppy awoke and ran under the table.
5. The dog stood looking up and barking.	Amy couldn't find her backpack.
6. The wind slammed the door shut.	The squirrel scurried up the tree.

▶ **Rewrite three of the matched causes and effects as sentences. Use *because* or *so* to connect the cause and effect.**

7. _____

_____

8. _____

_____

9. _____

_____

UNIT I Friendship • **Lesson 2** *Angel Child, Dragon Child*

►The /e/ Sound

Rhyming Strategy Replace the underlined word in each sentence with a rhyming word from the box that makes sense in the sentence.

bread	spent	sweater	next	send

1. I <u>sent</u> too much money at the fair. _____

2. Would you like some butter on your <u>head</u>? _____

3. We are going to Florida <u>text</u> year. _____

4. Be sure to wear your <u>better</u> tonight. _____

5. I <u>bend</u> my grandma my school picture every year. _____

Proofreading Strategy Circle the four spelling mistakes in the paragraph. Then write the misspelled words correctly on the lines.

Every summer, my parents sind me to camp. I have so much fun there. Last year, we set up a tend on the ege of a lake. I shared a tent with my friends. I can't wait to see thim again.

_____

_____

_____

SPELLING

UNIT 1 **Friendship • Lesson 2** *Angel Child, Dragon Child*

▶Context Clues

▶ **Circle the context clues in each sentence that help you learn the meaning of the underlined word.**

1. The <u>curious</u> cat peeked through the window to see what was there.

2. He was so <u>furious</u> that he pounded his fist on the table and yelled.

3. He felt <u>forlorn</u> when he lost his hamster and cried all day.

4. Dana was so <u>baffled</u> by the mystery that she could not figure it out.

5. The <u>jovial</u> man laughed and told jokes.

6. Seth was so <u>jittery</u> that he jumped when the doorbell rang.

▶ **Write sentences for the words below. Include context clues to show the meaning of each word.**

1. pleased _____

2. sweet _____

3. patient _____

VOCABULARY

UNIT I Friendship • **Lesson 2** *Angel Child, Dragon Child*

▶Pronouns

Circle the pronouns in the paragraph below.

Queen Victoria of England made a special friend, Sarah Forbes Bonetta, who was only six years old when she came to England. Her story began in Africa. It was a tale of courage. She had special marks on her face. They showed her to be a princess. Then she went to live with the queen of England, Queen Victoria. Imagine the change for her from Africa! The queen liked Sarah very much because she was a smart and lively child. Sarah moved into Windsor Castle with the Phipps family. It is one of the biggest and oldest castles in England. Queen Victoria visited them frequently. Then the queen thought Sarah's health might be harmed by the cold in Britain, so she sent her back to Africa to attend school. She went to Sierra Leone. It had an English school for girls. Later, the queen called her back to England because of war in Sierra Leone. When the war ended, Sarah returned to Africa, married, and became a teacher. To learn more about the queen and her special friend, read *At Her Majesty's Request,* by Walter Myers. It is an interesting book, and he is a good writer.

▶Compare and Contrast

We all like our friends because in some ways we are alike and in other ways we are very different. What colors do you like? What is your favorite food? Which animals do you like? Where do you like to go? Use the diagram below to tell about you and your friend. Write words that tell how you are different in the circle on the left. Write words that tell how your friend is different in the circle on the right. Write words that tell how both of you are alike in the middle, where the two circles overlap.

COMPREHENSION

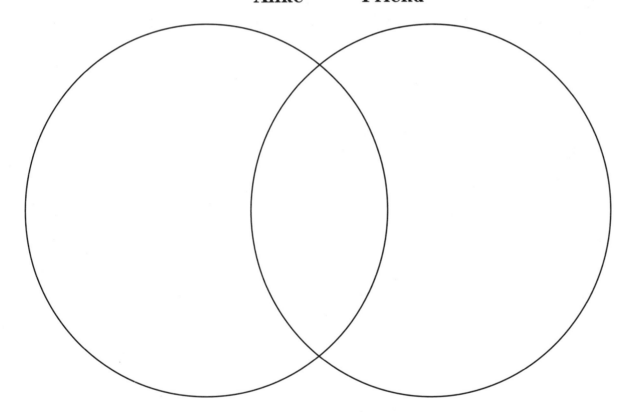

| You | Both Alike | Your Friend |

On another piece of paper write two sentences telling why you chose this person to be your friend.

UNIT I   Friendship • **Lesson 3** *The Tree House*

SPELLING

▶ The /i/ Sound

Rhyming Word Strategy Write two words that rhyme with each word below.

1. grip _____

2. trick _____

3. lift _____

4. stitch _____

Visualization Strategy Write the correct spelling for each word. Then use each word in a sentence.

1. brik _____

_____

2. fenish _____

_____

3. windou _____

_____

4. viset _____

_____

5. felm _____

_____

UNIT 1   Friendship • **Lesson 3** *The Tree House*

▶Word Structure

For each word, take off the prefix or suffix and write the base word. Then write the meaning of the base word on the line.

1. unforgivable _____

2. kindness _____

3. helplessness _____

4. repainted _____

5. misunderstand _____

6. friendly _____

7. talking _____

8. happiness _____

VOCABULARY

▶Verbs

Verbs can express action—what the subject does or what is done to the subject—or a state of being—what the subject is. In this first exercise, rewrite the action verb sentence as a linking verb sentence, and vice-versa. Example: *Pee Wee and Jackie became friends* is turned into *Pee Wee and Jackie are people who became friends*.

1. Lewis Carroll wrote *Alice in Wonderland.*

_____

2. She is the person who talked with the March Hare.

_____

3. The March Hare was always in a hurry.

_____

4. Alice fell down a rabbit hole into Wonderland.

_____

Some action verbs express actions you can see, and others express actions you cannot. After each sentence, write *S* (seen) or *U* (unseen), depending on whether the verb's action can be seen or not.

1. Carroll sailed on the river with Alice Lidell and her friends. _____

2. He thought up stories about them and a talking rabbit. _____

3. He told them the stories to pass the time. _____

4. They wanted more and more stories. _____

Name _____ Date _____

▶ Topic Sentences

Write a topic sentence for each main idea below. Then write at least three details or reasons that support the idea in your topic sentence.

Main idea: learning is fun

_____

_____

_____

_____

Main idea: food that is good for you

_____

_____

_____

_____

Main idea: food that is bad for you

_____

_____

_____

_____

WRITER'S CRAFT

▶The /o/ Sound

 Proofreading Strategy Circle the misspelled word in each sentence. Then write the correct spelling on the line.

1. I can't see the klock from here. _____

2. There were lotz of animals on the farm. _____

3. A floke of birds flew over our heads. _____

4. I'll meet you in the hotel loby. _____

5. What a great spott for a picnic! _____

 Visualization Strategy Circle the correct spelling for each word. Then write it on the line.

1. boddy	bodi	body	_____
2. shot	schot	shote	_____
3. stoking	stockin	stocking	_____
4. jobe	job	jobb	_____
5. crop	cropp	croup	_____

SPELLING

UNIT I Friendship • **Lesson 4** *Rugby & Rosie*

►Using a Dictionary

►Look at each pair of words. Choose a word from the box that would be found on a dictionary page with each of the guide words. Write the word on the line.

indoor	yeast	recess	picnic	depth

1. pick/pictograph _____

2. yard/yellowbird _____

3. deport/deputy _____

4. indiscreet/induct _____

5. recant/recharge _____

►Write a definition for each word below.

6. error _____

7. melt _____

8. giant _____

VOCABULARY

▶Verb Phrases

Verb phrases are made up of helping verbs and main verbs.

Some helping verbs tell you the verb tense. For these sentences, circle the helping verb if it shows the past, underline it if it shows the present, and bracket it if it shows the future.

1. Dogs are helping many people in need.

2. Dogs have rescued people.

3. A German shepherd was honored by the mayor for saving people during a flood.

4. A dog has gone into a burning building to save lives.

5. Dogs are cheering up patients in hospitals.

6. Usually, cheery patients will heal faster.

7. Dogs are bringing many benefits to our lives.

8. Dogs will continue to bring benefits to our lives.

Write in the helping verb according to the instruction at the end of the sentence.

9. Other animals _____ help people also. (ability)

10. A rooster _____ wake you up in the morning. (possibility)

11. A cat _____ scare the mice from a farmer's barn. (willingness)

12. Some animals _____ be trained to learn to help people. (necessity)

UNIT I Friendship • **Lesson 4** *Rugby & Rosie*

▶Sentence Variety

▶The following paragraph has only short, choppy sentences. Rewrite the paragraph so there is a good mix of short and long sentences.

My name is Ben. I am a fourth grader. I go to Peachtree Elementary. I like school. I like math. I am good in science. I am good in music.

_____

_____

_____

_____

▶Now write a paragraph about yourself. Use a variety of short and long sentences.

_____

_____

_____

_____

_____

_____

WRITER'S CRAFT

UNIT 1 ▶ Friendship • **Lesson 5** *Teammates*

▶ Main Idea and Supporting Details

COMPREHENSION

Plan a paragraph about the topic *My Dream Vacation*. Use the word map below to help you organize your ideas. Write your main idea on the word map. Next, add the details. Add extra details to the word map if you wish. Then, on another sheet of paper, write a topic sentence from your main idea. Write a detail sentence for each detail on your word map.

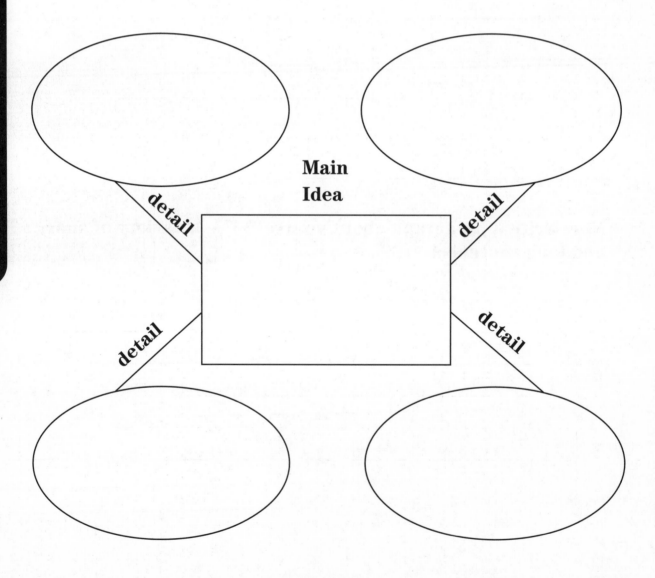

▶The /u/ Sound

 Consonant Substitution Strategy Make two or more new words by changing the underlined letter or letters in each word. Then write a sentence using one of the new words.

1. <u>b</u>lush _____

_____

2. <u>b</u>ut _____

_____

3. <u>c</u>rust _____

_____

4. <u>d</u>ump _____

_____

5. <u>g</u>ruff _____

_____

 Visualization Strategy Write the correct spelling for each misspelled word. Then use each word in a sentence.

1. skrub _____

_____

2. thumpp _____

_____

▶Using a Thesaurus

VOCABULARY

▶**For each word below, write another word that means the same thing. Look in a thesaurus if you need help.**

1. rage _____

2. rear _____

3. shut _____

4. fetch _____

5. correct _____

▶**Think of a synonym for each word below. Write a sentence using the synonym.**

1. own _____

2. draft _____

3. timid _____

4. hound _____

5. humorous _____

▶ Types of Sentences

Time capsules contain special items that tell about people and events from the time the capsule was buried. Imagine you have been given the job of picking the items to go into a time capsule to be opened one hundred years from now.

▶ **Write a declarative sentence about something you would pick.**

_____

▶ **Write an interrogative sentence that is a question you want to ask people one hundred years in the future.**

_____

▶ **Write an imperative sentence about something you think people will still be doing in one hundred years, but that you want people to stop doing.**

_____

▶ **Write an exclamatory sentence showing how you think people will react to what you put in the time capsule.**

_____

GRAMMAR

UNIT I   Friendship • **Lesson 5** *Teammates*

WRITER'S CRAFT

▶Staying on Topic

The information below is enough for two paragraphs. Put a 1 next to the information you think belongs in the first paragraph. Put a 2 next to the information you think belongs in the second paragraph. Look at all the information numbered 1 and decide what the main idea is. Write a topic sentence. Repeat for paragraph 2.

_____ plants make their own food

_____ grow plants from seeds

_____ all plants need air, sunlight, water, and warmth

_____ grow plants from parts of the plant

_____ plants stay in one place

_____ green beans, radishes, peppers

_____ plants have cells to help them stand upright

_____ potatoes and pineapples

_____

_____

_____

UNIT 1 Friendship • **Lesson 6** *The Legend of Damon and Pythias*

▶ Short Vowel Sounds

 Meaning Strategy Fill in the blank with a word from the box that best completes each sentence.

prison	robbers	struggle	read	candy

1. I _____ a story in the paper today.

2. Some _____ stole money from a _____ store.

3. The police came and there was a _____.

4. Everything worked out and now the robbers are in _____ .

 Rhyming Strategy Replace the underlined word in each sentence with a rhyming word from the box that makes sense in the sentence.

top	brand	best	jump	hobby

1. You are my <u>rest</u> friend. _____

2. Do you <u>stump</u> rope? _____

3. What <u>land</u> of cereal should I buy? _____

4. Collecting stickers is a fun <u>lobby</u>. _____

5. We climbed to the <u>stop</u> of the hill. _____

SPELLING

▶ Vocabulary Strategies

VOCABULARY

Circle the word that has nearly the same meaning as each underlined word.

1. Many fish live in the <u>sea</u>.

   valleys   mountains   ocean

2. <u>Eagles</u> fly around the highlands.

   fish   leopards   birds

3. Sometimes you can spot a mother and her <u>lambs</u>.

   babies   family   mates

4. You might even see a whole <u>drove</u> of sheep.

   couple   group   car

5. The <u>climate</u> can be very cold.

   ocean   weather   mountain

6. Some mountains have an <u>altitude</u> of thousands of feet.

   width   depth   height

UNIT 1   Friendship • **Lesson 6** *The Legend of Damon and Pythias*

▶Review

Write the capital over any letter that should be capitalized, underline subject pronouns, circle object pronouns, put an *X* over helping verbs, and fill in the proper end punctuation. Do not mark possessive pronouns.

cesar chavez was known as the "farmworker's friend" He was born on march 31, 1927 in yuma, arizona Cesar's family was happy, and his father worked hard for them He owned a grocery store. cesar's mother worked hard for them also cesar helped her out as well she was his inspiration. Then the depression came, and they lost the store. what were they to do They became migrant workers. migrant workers have hard lives their lives are spent traveling from place to place picking vegetables and fruits for not much money Cesar knew then that he would help them have better lives. How would he do that When he grew up, he, dolores huerta, and others started the united farmworkers in california It is a union, which works to make the lives of migrant workers better

UNIT 2 City Wildlife • **Lesson I** *The Boy Who Didn't Believe in Spring*

▶The /âr/ and /ar/ Sounds

SPELLING

Visualization Strategy Circle the correct spelling for each spelling word. Then write it on the line.

1. dare   dayr   dair   _____

2. chare   chear   chair   _____

3. wayre   wear   wair   _____

4. started   stearted   sterted   _____

5. apeartments apartmints apartments _____

Rhyming Strategy Write two words that have the same spelling pattern and rhyme with each word below.

1. pair _____

2. tear _____

3. care _____

4. star _____

5. shark _____

The /âr/ and /ar/ Sounds • Challenge

Antonyms

▶ **Write two antonyms that mean the opposite of each word below.**

1. alert _____

2. laugh _____

3. rude _____

4. far _____

▶ **Write a word on the line that is an antonym for each word. Then use it in a sentence.**

1. light _____

2. new _____

3. loud _____

4. enemy _____

5. fix _____

VOCABULARY

UNIT 2 City Wildlife • **Lesson I** *The Boy Who Didn't Believe in Spring*

▶Quotation Marks

When writing dialogue (a conversation between two people), put quotation marks around the speaker's exact words.

Put the following dialogue between city animals in its correct order of response and add quotation marks. Start with the worm.

1. I break down plant material to feed the soil, said the worm.

2. We fly in a beautiful V-shape, the goose said to the bee.

3. Why do you fly in a V-shape? the blue jay asked the goose.

4. The bee said to the worm, I pollinate the flowers.

_____

_____

_____

_____

_____

_____

_____

_____

_____

▶Time and Order Words

Think about the steps you go through when you brush your
teeth, beginning with when you pick up your toothbrush, until
you put your brush back down. Write about the process you
use. Use time and order words to clarify the order of the steps.

_____

_____

_____

_____

_____

_____

_____

_____

_____

_____

_____

_____

_____

_____

WRITER'S CRAFT

▶ Drawing Conclusions

▶ **Read each conclusion. Draw a line to match it with the information that would result in drawing that conclusion.**

Information	Conclusions
1. Stevie was still in bed when the bus passed his house.	Running a race is tiring.
2. Everyone cheered and crowded around Brenda.	The race car engine was ruined.
3. Mary sat down to catch her breath.	He will be late for school.
4. The book slipped out of Carla's hands and into a mud puddle.	She scored the winning point.
5. Smoke was rising up into the air.	She would have to buy a new book.

▶ **Read each conclusion. Write two information sentences to support the conclusion.**

6. There was a violent thunderstorm.

_____

_____

7. Squirrels are living in the attic.

_____

_____

COMPREHENSION

▶The /er/ and /or/ Sounds

 Proofreading Strategy Circle the word that is misspelled in each sentence. Then spell the word correctly on the line.

1. We have a swing on our pourch. _____

2. My sister is a nerse at a hospital. _____

3. Don't forgit to bring your books tomorrow. _____

4. I had to herry, so I wouldn't miss my bus. _____

5. My pet burd is blue, red, and yellow. _____

 Visualization Strategy Write the correct spelling for each misspelled word.

1. bern _____

2. stourm _____

3. hert _____

4. befour _____

5. erban _____

SPELLING

▶Categories

Put some animal words in the correct categories.

Animals

Land   **Air**   **Water**

Example   dog   dove   trout

_____   _____   _____

_____   _____   _____

_____   _____   _____

VOCABULARY

▶ Commas in a Series

▶ **Pick a word or phrase from the following list and write it in the appropriate series, being sure to add commas:** *in cities, grey fox, foxes live in dens, on golf courses, Fox babies are called kits, the kits,* **and** *cars.*

1. The red fox _____ and Arctic fox are three kinds of foxes.

2. Foxes live in fields in the woods and _____.

3. _____ goat babies are called *kids* and kangaroo babies are called *joeys*.

4. City foxes live in parks _____ and around baseball fields.

5. Birds live in nests gophers live in holes and _____.

6. A den has room for _____ a mommy and a daddy.

7. City foxes must be careful of _____ buses and trucks.

▶ **Commas in a series can separate single words, phrases, and sentences. Identify each of the sentences about foxes in this way.**

1. _____   5. _____

2. _____   6. _____

3. _____   7. _____

4. _____

MECHANICS

WRITER'S CRAFT

▶Organizing Expository Text

Read each of the following main ideas. Write a topic sentence for each one. Then use events to tell more about the main idea. Make sure the events are in the order they happened or should happen. Finally, write a closing sentence.

1. getting ready to take a test

_____

_____

_____

_____

2. things you have learned

_____

_____

_____

_____

3. having a friend over to play

_____

_____

_____

_____

Fantasy and Reality

The author of "Make Way for Ducklings" did a lot of research and observation to learn facts about real ducks before he wrote his fantasy. Choose an animal, perhaps your own pet, and write a fantasy story based on the facts you know about the animal.

Do you have a cat that likes to climb trees? Could the cat become a famous mountain climber or be an acrobat in a circus? Do you have a dog that is very protective? Could the dog be a brave knight who defends people? Could a turtle, going in and out of its shell, be a secret, undercover spy? Perhaps three chirping crickets could start their own band. Maybe a goldfish could be a deep-sea diver looking for sunken treasure.

Try one of these ideas or one of your own, and have fun! Use more paper if you need more room to write.

_____

_____

_____

_____

_____

_____

_____

_____

COMPREHENSION

SPELLING

▶The Final /əl/ Sound

Visualization Strategy Write a word from the box that has the same spelling as the underlined parts of each word.

little	pebble	jungle	candle

1. ta<u>ngle</u> _____

2. ha<u>ndle</u> _____

3. bo<u>ttle</u> _____

4. bu<u>bble</u> _____

Proofreading Strategy Circle the misspelled word in each sentence. Then write the correct spelling on the line.

1. Have you seen a duck waddal? _____

2. I have a marbel that is green and white. _____

3. She eats an appel with lunch every day. _____

4. My parrot likes to whistel a song. _____

5. I want to swim with the sea turtals. _____

UNIT 2 City Wildlife • **Lesson 3** *Make Way for Ducklings*

 # Synonyms

**Choose a word from the box that is a synonym for each word.
Use each word in a sentence.**

| strike | complete | possess | decrease | dash | Earth |

1. finish _____

2. lessen _____

3. hit _____

4. own _____

5. world _____

6. run _____

VOCABULARY

▶Commas in Dialogue

MECHANICS

▶Some of these sentences use the comma correctly and some do not. Make any needed corrections by filling in or crossing out commas.

1. "Where do butterflies come from?" asked Clarrisa.

2. "They come from eggs," Jesse answered.

3. Clarrisa asked "They hatch from eggs?"

4. Jesse responded "They come out of a cocoon."

5. "Where does the cocoon come from?", Clarrisa asked.

6. "From the caterpillar", said Jesse.

▶Sometimes the dialogue continues after the speaker is named. Fill in commas where you think they should go.

1. "When the caterpillar spins the cocoon" Ms. Morales said "it is called a *pupa.*"

2. "The cocoon is like a hard shell" she continued. "The butterfly comes out of the cocoon."

3. "Does anyone know what else the pupa is called?" she asked. "It's called a chrysalis."

4. "Nature is amazing!" said Danesha in delight. "Imagine making a butterfly!"

5. "That's right, Danesha" said Ms. Morales "nature can really make a person wonder."

▶ **Paragraph Form**

▶ **Choose a wild animal to research. You may use encyclopedias, magazines, or the Internet to gather information to complete the outline below. Each section that begins with a roman numeral will be a paragraph.**

Name of Animal: _____

I. Description of the Animal

A. Body Covering and Size

1. _____   2. _____

B. How the Animal Moves

1. _____   2. _____

C. Any Special Characteristics

1. _____   2. _____

II. Habitat

A. Environment

1. _____   2. _____

B. Shelter

1. _____   2. _____

C. Food

1. _____   2. _____

▶ **On a separate sheet of paper, write two paragraphs using the notes you wrote.**

WRITER'S CRAFT

▶The /ow/ Sound

 Rhyming Strategy Write two or more words that rhyme with each word below.

1. blouse _____

2. mound _____

3. down _____

 Proofreading Strategy Circle the five misspelled words in the paragraph. Then write the correct spellings of the words on the lines.

Water surounds the Florida Keys. They are beautiful islands in southe Florida. It is hard to counte all the people who visit the Keys. There is always a croud. It's a nice place to visit threwout the year.

_____

_____

_____

_____

_____

▶Word Concept

Read the paragraph and answer the questions that follow.

It is important to have good nutrition. When eaten, nutritious foods give people energy and help fight sickness. You can have good nutrition by eating certain foods. It is best to eat foods like fruit and vegetables to keep healthy.

1. What is the concept of good nutrition?

    _____

2. What words give context clues about the meaning of good nutrition?

    _____

    _____

    _____

    _____

VOCABULARY

UNIT 2 City Wildlife • **Lesson 4** *Urban Roosts*

▶Capitalization of Places

MECHANICS

Imagine that you are a particular city animal. You have lived all over the world. Write a letter to a friend explaining to him or her the best and worst places to live, and why. Make up imaginary places and facts about them, if you wish. Be sure to advise your friend on a number of places, and capitalize the name of each of them.

_____

_____

_____

_____

_____

_____

_____

_____

_____

_____

_____

_____

_____

_____

_____

_____

Capitalization of Places • Challenge

▶ Topic Sentences

▶ You are going to write two or three paragraphs about your city, town, or village. First make a list of things you can tell about. Then decide which things in your list will go into each paragraph. For example, points of interest or landmarks might go in one paragraph. Then write topic sentences for each of your paragraphs.

My Town

_____   _____   _____

_____   _____   _____

_____   _____   _____

_____   _____   _____

Topic sentence for first paragraph: _____

_____

Topic sentence for second paragraph: _____

_____

Topic sentence for third paragraph: _____

_____

▶ Now, on a separate sheet of paper, fill in detail sentences for each of your paragraphs. Add illustrations with captions.

WRITER'S CRAFT

▶Cause and Effect

COMPREHENSION

▶**Read the following causes and effects. Draw a line to match causes with their effects.**

Causes	Effects
1. Myrna was running late.	He put out extra food.
2. Ted noticed the cat had kittens now.	She forgot her homework.
3. Tina seemed sad today.	The rug was soaked.
4. The window was open all day.	The flower grew.
5. Mia watered it every day.	Keesha smiled at her.

▶**Read each effect. Write a sentence for each to explain the cause.**

6. **The king declared a holiday.**

_____

_____

7. **They built a special house for bluebirds.**

_____

_____

▶ The /oi/ Sound

Consonant Substitution Strategy Make one or more new words by changing the first letter in each word. Then write a sentence using one of the words.

1. point _____

_____

2. coil _____

_____

3. join _____

_____

4. loyal _____

_____

5. boy _____

_____

Visualization Strategy Circle the correct spelling for each word. Then write it on the line.

1. broile   broyal   broil   _____

2. poison   poisen   poisan   _____

3. injoy   enjoi   enjoy   _____

4. royale   roil   royal   _____

SPELLING

▶ Homophones

▶ Complete each sentence with the correct homophone pair from the box.

ball	bawl	knight	night	plane	plain	fair	fare

1. How much was the _____ at the county _____?

2. Did he _____ when he was hit by the _____?

3. The _____ only left the castle at _____ .

4. She wore _____ clothes on the _____ .

▶ Write a sentence for each pair of words.

1. horse, hoarse _____

_____

2. ad, add _____

_____

3. find, fined _____

_____

4. blue, blew _____

_____

VOCABULARY

▶Question Marks and Exclamation Points

▶Write down three questions you want to ask the deer in *Two Days in May* about its life.

_____

_____

_____

▶When the question mark or exclamation point is part of a speaker's exact words, put it inside quotation marks. If it is not, put it outside the quotation marks.

1. Have you read "The Raven"

2. Whatever you do, don't yell "Uncle"

3. "What time is it" she asked.

4. "Stop" he shouted.

5. Have you read "The Fish That Got Away"

6. Joey exclaimed, "Look at the beautiful fawn"

▶Define what an interrogative sentence is.

_____

_____

MECHANICS

▶Audience and Purpose

WRITER'S CRAFT

▶ Write a short sentence to persuade your classmates to start a garden at your school.

_____

_____

_____

▶ Rewrite that sentence to persuade your principal to let you start a garden at your school.

_____

_____

_____

▶ Rewrite that sentence one more time to entertain your teacher with a story about starting a garden at your school.

_____

_____

_____

Name _____ Date _____

▶ Author's Purpose

An author's purpose can be to entertain, inform, explain, or persuade the reader. Sometimes there can be more than just one purpose. "Secret Place" was written to entertain and inform.

▶ **Write two sentences to persuade people to create nature sanctuaries in the city.**

_____

_____

_____

▶ **Write two sentences to explain why the place had to be a secret.**

_____

_____

_____

▶ **Write three or four sentences to inform others about wildlife in the city and disappearing habitats. You may use an encyclopedia, a book from the school library, or the Internet to find information.**

_____

_____

_____

COMPREHENSION

▶ Unit 2 Review

SPELLING

 Rhyming Strategy Write a word that has the same spelling pattern and rhymes with each word below.

1. growl _____

2. return _____

3. pear _____

4. choice _____

5. puddle _____

 Visualization Strategy Circle the correct spelling for each word. Then write it on the line.

1. growch   groch   grouch   _____

2. jangald   jengled   jangled   _____

3. corner   cornor   cornur   _____

4. durt   dirt   dert   _____

5. noyse   noize   noise   _____

UNIT 2 City Wildlife • **Lesson 6** *Secret Place*

▶Unit 2 Review

▶Write whether each pair of words are synonyms, antonyms, or homophones.

1. shallow/deep _____

2. hair/hare _____

3. stop/halt _____

4. empty/full _____

5. put/place _____

6. flower/flour _____

▶Write a pair of synonyms, antonyms, and homophones of your own.

1. Synonyms _____

2. Antonyms _____

3. Homophones _____

VOCABULARY

▶Review

Put in capitals, commas, quotation marks, question marks, and exclamation points as needed.

Before coming to live on top of a tall office building in cincinnati, ohio, in the united states, the peregrine falcons traveled through canada new york state and pittsburgh. What a long trip They played hunted and talked along the way. And they had plenty of time to talk with each other. What do you think they said

Look down there Fred squawked as they were leaving canada. It's niagara falls.

Wow It is so big and noisy Frieda squawked back in excitement.

The map says we should turn right over new york the allegheny mountains and pennsylvania Fred shouted over the loud wind.

Frieda exclaimed in exasperation Now, who has heard of peregrine falcons needing a map

Fred asked But how will we know where we are

Frieda answered We follow our instincts.

Oh, that's right Fred answered. I forgot.

MECHANICS

▶Effective Beginnings

▶ Write a good beginning for a personal narrative. Using the different ways to write good beginnings for nonfiction given below, write five different beginnings for your narrative.

▶ Ask a question.

_____

_____

▶ Tell something that happened to you or someone else.

_____

_____

▶ Use an interesting or surprising fact.

_____

_____

▶ Use a quote.

_____

_____

▶ State a problem.

_____

_____

UNIT 3 Imagination • **Lesson 1** *Through Grandpa's Eyes*

▶The /ā/ Sound

Rhyming Strategy Write two or more words that rhyme with each word below.

1. stay _____

2. main _____

3. sail _____

Consonant-Substitution Strategy Make as many words as you can by adding the letters in the box to each word ending.

fl	bl	sp	pl	sh

1. -ame _____

2. -aze _____

3. -ade _____

4. -ate _____

5. -ace _____

6. -ake _____

SPELLING

Name _____ Date _____

▶Base Word Families

▶Write the base word for each pair below.

1. quicker, quickly _____

2. childish, children _____

3. overpriced, pricing _____

4. motherly, motherhood _____

5. sharpen, sharper _____

▶For each word below, write two words that belong to its family.

1. dark _____

2. laugh _____

3. write _____

4. scare _____

5. agree _____

VOCABULARY

▶Sensory Adjectives

Adjectives describe things, and sensory adjectives ask us to imagine things with the five senses: sight, hearing, touch, smell, and taste.

Write the sensory adjective that describes the subject of each sentence. Choose from the following list; each word is used only once: *loud, heavy, light, hot, red, sweet, bright, cold, soft, beautiful, stinky, salty,* **and** *furry.*

1. This elephant weighs a ton. _____

2. The steam from that volcano will burn. _____

3. I can't hear you because the music is turned up. _____

4. Look at the color of the fire engine. _____

5. The sun is so strong I can hardly see. _____

6. This feather hardly weighs anything at all. _____

7. Yum! This apple tastes like candy. _____

8. Ugh! That old fish really smells! _____

9. Hmm. That rose is so pretty. _____

10. The inside of the refrigerator will make you shiver. _____

11. These chips really have a lot of salt on them. _____

12. The cloth feels gentle on my skin. _____

13. That beaver has a long, thick coat. _____

UNIT 3 Imagination • **Lesson I** *Through Grandpa's Eyes*

▶Descriptive Details

Imagine a big plate of hot spaghetti. Make a list of words or phrases you think of when you imagine it. Then write a description for someone who has never seen spaghetti. Remember to use your senses to describe as much as you can.

_____

_____

_____

_____

_____

_____

_____

_____

_____

_____

_____

_____

_____

_____

_____

WRITER'S CRAFT

▶ Fantasy and Reality

COMPREHENSION

Read the beginnings of the sentences that follow. Add your own ending to create complete sentences that could be part of a fantasy story. Remember that fantasies are about things that could not happen in real life.

1. Tammy and her classmates headed out for the woods _____

_____

2. The children gathered around to hear _____

_____

3. The sky was blue, but the wind was stirring the trees because ____

_____

4. All of a sudden, Micah turned around and saw _____

_____

5. The deer and rabbits _____

_____

6. She shined the flashlight into the cave and saw _____

_____

7. When Thomas looked up into the sky, _____

_____

UNIT 3 Imagination • **Lesson 2** *The Cat Who Became a Poet*

▶The /ē/ Sound

 Visualization Strategy Circle the correct spelling for each word. Then write it on the line.

1. easey   easy   easee   _____

2. beaste   beest   beast   _____

3. cleen   clean   cleane   _____

4. hearing   heering   hearring   _____

5. creck   creeke   creek   _____

 Pronunciation Strategy Circle the words in each sentence that have the /ē/ sound. Underline the letters that spell the /ē/ sound.

1. Sam lives on my street.

2. I have seen him riding his bike.

3. There is a huge tree in my back yard.

4. I keep my diary in it.

5. I like to eat hamburgers and fries.

SPELLING

UNIT 3 Imagination • **Lesson 2** *The Cat Who Became a Poet*

▶Suffixes

VOCABULARY

▶Add two of the suffixes in the box to each word to make two new words. Write them on the lines.

-ness	-ly	-ful	-less

1. hope _____

2. short _____

3. care _____

4. thought _____

5. kind _____

▶Write a word of your own for each suffix.

6. -ness _____

7. -ly _____

8. -ful _____

9. -less _____

Name _____ Date _____

▶ Contractions

▶ **Sometimes contractions are confused with words that sound like them. Write in the correct choice from the pair at the end of each sentence about a space scientist. (Science uses imagination too.)**

1. "_____ a good day for a space flight," Ellen Ochoa thought. (It's/Its)

2. "I bet _____ going to launch today." (they're/their)

3. The space shuttle had _____ engines working well. (its/it's)

4. "_____ going up today," her commander said. (We're/Wear)

5. He pointed to the sky, "Let's hop in and go _____." (there/they're)

▶ **In this story about the scientist Ernest Just, write the correct contractions made from the words in this list:** *could not, I will, he would, I am, was not, you are.*

Ernest Just always believed _____ be a scientist.

He _____ one to believe he _____ do something

he set his mind to. And guess what? When he was a boy

living by the ocean, he said to himself, "_____ study

hard so _____ able to be a marine biologist." His

mother said to him proudly, "With that determination,

_____ going to go far."

USAGE

UNIT 3 Imagination • **Lesson 2** *The Cat Who Became a Poet*

WRITER'S CRAFT

▶Using the Sounds of Words

▶ **Make a list of special words that could be used to describe things that go on in your classroom. You should list words for sounds, repeated beginning consonant sounds, repeated words, and rhyming words.**

_____

_____

_____

_____

_____

▶ **Write a paragraph or short poem about activities in your classroom, using words and phrases from your list.**

_____

_____

_____

_____

_____

_____

_____

_____

UNIT 3 Imagination • **Lesson 3** *A Cloak for the Dreamer*

▶Making Inferences

Read the following paragraph. Think about the information in the paragraph and what you already know. Then write out all the inferences you can make from the paragraph.

It was so early in the morning that the sun had not even come out yet. Josh took out his key and opened the door. Inside the familiar room, he found his way to the light switch in the dark. As the light came on, it shined on the containers that held all the ingredients he would work with today. He reached for his recipe book, tied his apron, and began his work. In just a few hours, customers would be lined up outside, drawn by the tempting smells of fresh bread and pastries.

_____

_____

_____

_____

_____

_____

_____

_____

_____

UNIT 3 Imagination • **Lesson 3** *A Cloak for the Dreamer*

▶The /ī/ Sound

Rhyming Strategy Choose the word from the box that rhymes with each word below. Then use the word in a sentence.

glide	time	fine	pipe	sight

1. light _____

2. line _____

3. slide _____

4. ripe _____

5. dime _____

Proofreading Strategy Circle the misspelled words in each sentence. Then write the words correctly on the lines.

1. That lite is bright!   _____

2. He has a great smyle.   _____

3. The loud noise gave me a frite. _____

4. I don't like hie places.   _____

5. How wyde is the TV?   _____

SPELLING

▶ Prefixes

Write a word with a prefix in place of each of the words below. Then use the new word in a sentence.

1. heat again _____

   _____

2. twice a month _____

   _____

3. three wheeled bike _____

   _____

4. not able _____

   _____

5. not honest _____

   _____

6. count wrong _____

   _____

VOCABULARY

▶Verb Tenses

The tense of the verb tells whether the sentence takes
place in the past, present, or future.

▶**Pretend you are the teacher, and you are going to test the
class on verb tenses. Write three sentences—one in the past,
one in the present, and one in the future tense—for students
to identify the verb tense.**

1. _____

2. _____

3. _____

▶**The second verb should be in the same tense as the first
verb. Circle the correct second verb based on the tense of
the underlined, first verb.**

1. Susan McKinney Steward <u>thought</u> that she was/is
   smart enough to be a doctor.

2. Many men in 1865 <u>believed</u> women are/were not smart
   enough to be doctors.

3. Her professors <u>said</u> she worked/will work hard for
   her success.

4. Steward <u>felt</u> proud when she becomes/became the
   first black woman doctor in New York.

USAGE

▶Place and Location Words

Write directions to guide your audience from your school to your house using place and location words.

_____

_____

_____

_____

_____

_____

_____

_____

_____

_____

_____

_____

_____

_____

_____

_____

_____

WRITER'S CRAFT

UNIT 3 Imagination • **Lesson 4** *Picasso*

COMPREHENSION

▶Compare and Contrast

▶The following sentences compare things that are alike in some way. Draw a line to match each part of the following animals to a description by a person with his or her eyes closed.

1. A pig's tail is like   a telephone pole.

2. A giraffe's neck is like   a boat oar.

3. A squirrel's tail is like   a tuba.

4. A beaver's tail is like   a corkscrew.

5. A ram's horn is like   a backscratcher.

6. A chicken's leg is like   a feather duster.

▶Now, close your eyes and think of an animal. What objects do you think of as you imagine the animal? Complete each of the sentences. Then, ask a classmate to read your sentences and guess what animal you are describing.

7. Its nose is like _____.

8. Its tail is like _____.

9. Its ear is like _____.

10. Its leg is like _____.

11. Its body is like _____.

12. It is a _____.

▶The /ō/ Sound

 Meaning Strategy Write a sentence for each spelling word below.

1. goal _____

2. vote _____

3. froze _____

4. coal _____

5. alone _____

6. soap _____

 Consonant-Substitution Strategy Make two new words by changing the underlined letter or letters in each word.

1. <u>c</u>one _____

2. <u>sp</u>oke _____

3. <u>ch</u>ose _____

4. <u>m</u>ost _____

Name _____ Date _____

▶ Multiple Meanings

VOCABULARY

▶Write two meanings for each word below. Look in a
dictionary if you need help.

1. kind _____

2. pen _____

3. rest _____

4. school _____

5. lie _____

6. bowl _____

▶Think of a word that has two different meanings. Write a
sentence using each meaning.

_____

_____

_____

Multiple Meanings • Challenge

▶ Plural Nouns

▶ Write a classified advertisement in which you list all the items you have for sale, along with your name, your phone number, and how much each item costs. You have more than one of each item, so put these in the plural: puppy, video game, hat, ax, monkey, latch, box, guppy, and bed.

_____

_____

_____

▶ In the space provided form the irregular plural of the word or words at the end of the sentence.

1. Indian farmers use _____ to pull ploughs. (ox)

2. Indian _____ believe cows are sacred. (person)

3. The Indian _____ would not work a cow hard. (man, woman, and child)

4. She had pet _____. (mouse)

5. The _____ were feeding by the lake. (goose, moose, and deer)

6. _____ are tools for eating. (Tooth)

USAGE

▶Figurative Language

WRITER'S CRAFT

▶ Read each of the following words. Then write a sentence containing a simile, a metaphor, and personification using each word.

1. sunshine   Simile: _____

          _____

          Metaphor: _____

          _____

          Personification: _____

          _____

2. flowers   Simile: _____

          _____

          Metaphor: _____

          _____

          Personification: _____

          _____

▶ Describe someone you know well using similes or metaphors. Underline the similes or metaphors you use.

_____

_____

UNIT 3 Imagination • **Lesson 5** *The Emperor's New Clothes*

▶Classify and Categorize

A Classified Puzzler

Look at the words in the box below. Write the words in the puzzle, grouped by season. Each word must be an item related to the season and fit in the spaces.

S _ _ _ _ _ _ _

_ _ _ _ _ _ U _ _

_ _ M _ _ _

_ _ _ _ _ M _ _ _ _

E _ _ _ _ _ _ _

_ R _ _ _

W _ _ _ _ _ _ _ _ _ _

_ I _ _ _ _ _

_ N _ _ _ _ _ _

T _ _ _ _ _ _ _

_ _ _ _ E _

_ _ _ R _

camper
earplugs
grass
mittens
scarf
shovel
snowgear
sunshine
swimsuit
toboggan
warm clothes
watermelon

COMPREHENSION

Challenge • *Classify and Categorize*   UNIT 3 • Lesson 5 **73**

UNIT 3 Imagination • **Lesson 5** *The Emperor's New Clothes*

▶The /o͞o/ and /u͞/ Sounds

Visualization Strategy Circle the correct spelling for each word. Then write it on the line.

1. doon   dune   dewn   duen   _____

2. loos   luese   lowse   loose   _____

3. chue   chew   chu   chewe   _____

4. rool   ruel   rule   roole   _____

Vowel-Substitution Strategy Fill in the blanks with the correct letters that spell a word from the box.

choose	flute	grew	few	scoop

1. The seeds gr_____ into a huge beanstalk.

2. Would you like a sc_____p of ice cream?

3. Emma plays the fl_____t_____ in the band.

4. There are only a f_____ days left until vacation.

5. It's hard to ch_____se from all the flavors.

SPELLING

Name _____ Date _____

▶Shades of Meaning

▶Complete the shades of meaning ranges below.

1. warm   _____

2. happy   _____

3. nervous   _____

4. smart   _____

5. damp   _____

▶Create two sets of your own shades of meaning ranges. Write them below.

_____

_____

VOCABULARY

UNIT 3 Imagination • **Lesson 5** *The Emperor's New Clothes*

▶Articles

The definite article—*the*—says that the noun refers to a particular person, place, or thing; the indefinite article—*a* or *an*—says the noun refers to a kind of person, place, or thing in general.

▶ **For the underlined words, substitute the suggested synonym and rewrite the sentence with the correct indefinite or definite article.**

1. Rafael was a <u>painter</u>. (artist)

   _____

2. He was an <u>Italian</u>. (man from Italy)

   _____

3. He was known as an <u>extremely well-mannered person</u>. (gentleman).

   _____

4. Rafael painted a <u>picture</u> of the Pope. (oil portrait)

   _____

▶ **Above any incorrect indefinite articles, write the definite article.**

An painting "School of Athens" is one of

Rafael's most important. In it a artist shows an

philosophers, mathematicians, and scholars of

ancient Athens.

▶Mood

▶ Choose a mood that you can create well. You may choose
suspense or humor. Begin by making a list of words or
phrases that you think of when you think of that mood.

_____   _____

_____   _____

_____   _____

_____   _____

▶ Keeping your mood in mind and using the words and phrases
you wrote down, write just the beginning of a story.

_____

_____

_____

_____

_____

_____

_____

_____

_____

WRITER'S CRAFT

▶ Author's Point of View

COMPREHENSION

"Roxaboxen" was written from the third-person point of view. Imagine you are one of the characters in the story. Are you Marion, handling serious city business as mayor? Are you Eleanor or Paul, competing to sell the best ice cream? Are you Jean or Anna May, baking yummy treats? Are you Jamie, giving Anna May another ticket for speeding? Perhaps you are Frances, slowly and carefully building the beautiful jeweled house of desert stones. Or are you Charles, building the biggest house in Roxaboxen? Write a story from the first-person point of view to tell about a wonderful day you spent in Roxaboxen. Do some planning on this page by writing some notes about what you want to say. Then, write your story on another sheet of paper.

_____

_____

_____

_____

_____

_____

_____

_____

_____

_____

_____

_____

UNIT 3 Imagination • **Lesson 6** *Roxaboxen*

▶Unit 3 Review

 Proofreading Strategy Circle the five misspelled words in the paragraph. Then write the misspelled words correctly on the lines.

Many of the jewls people wear are made of a precious ston . Eech stone is mayd of an element, such as oxygen or carbon. It is hard to believe these brite stones started out as elements.

_____

_____

_____

_____

Pronunciation Strategy Write the word from the box with the same vowel spelling as each set of words.

sail	soon	like	boat	reach

1. bike   hike   _____

2. moon   balloon   _____

3. goat   moat   _____

4. mail   pail   _____

5. beach   teach   _____

SPELLING

UNIT 3 Imagination • **Lesson 6** *Roxaboxen*

▶ Unit 3 Review

VOCABULARY

▶ Write a word with each prefix below.

1. un- _____

2. re- _____

3. dis- _____

4. bi- _____

5. mis- _____

▶ Write a word with each suffix below. Then use each word in a sentence.

1. -ness _____

_____

2. -ly _____

_____

3. -ful _____

_____

4. -less _____

_____

UNIT 3 Imagination • **Lesson 6** *Roxaboxen*

▶Review

▶**Write down the rules for making these regular nouns plural.**

1. *Bird:* The **birds** woke up Natasha.

_____

_____

2. *Lunch:* Our school serves hot **lunches**.

_____

_____

▶**At the end of the sentence, change the verb tense according to the direction.**

3. Michelangelo painted the ceiling of the Sistine Chapel. (future)

_____

4. Beautiful pictures fill the huge ceiling. (past)

_____

▶**Fill in apostrophes and correct indefinite articles by writing above the incorrect article.**

5. An contraction is one word made from more than one word.

6. *Wasnt, shouldnt, cant,* and *dont* are examples of contractions.

USAGE

▶ Sentence Combining

WRITER'S CRAFT

Complete the second half of each compound sentence below.

1. Jacob woke up bright and early, but _____

_____

2. Keisha needs to study, or _____

_____

3. Makiah emptied the waste baskets, and _____

_____

4. Write two short sentences about something in your
    classroom.

_____

_____

5. Write two short sentences about how you spend your
    free time. Now write one sentence that combines the
    subjects of at least two of those sentences.

_____

_____

_____

_____

UNIT 4 Money • **Lesson 1** *A New Coat for Anna*

▶Double Consonants

Consonant Substitution Strategy
Choose a set of letters from the box to complete each word. Write the word on the line.

tt	bb	dd	mm	nn

1. la ___ er _____

2. po ___ er _____

3. ru ___ er _____

4. di ___ er _____

5. ha ___ er _____

Rhyming Word Strategy
Write a word from the box that rhymes with each word below.

button	tomorrow	scatter	better	summer

1. batter _____

2. letter _____

3. drummer _____

4. glutton _____

5. borrow _____

Name _____ Date _____

▶Base Word Families

▶Add prefixes and suffixes to the words below to make new words in the same base word family.

1. luck _____

2. forgive _____

3. heavy _____

4. smooth _____

5. please _____

▶Write two more sets of word families.

6. _____

7. _____

VOCABULARY

UNIT 4 Money • **Lesson I** *A New Coat for Anna*

▶ Prepositions

▶**Prepositions can tell you the direction or position of a noun. At the end of each sentence, write the preposition that is the opposite of the preposition in the sentence.**

1. Most people put their money in banks to keep it safe. _____

2. Inside every bank there is a vault. _____

3. Some vaults are under the ground. _____

4. You walk down many flights of stairs to reach them. _____

5. Often you walk with a guard. _____

6. You walk towards the vault. _____

7. Another guard may stand in front of the vault. _____

8. He or she stands near the money. _____

▶**A prepositional phrase is the preposition plus its noun and any words that modify the noun. That means a prepositional phrase can be very long. Underline the complete prepositional phrases in this paragraph.**

Throughout the human race's history, there have been many forms of money. People who live on the small Yap Islands in the tropical, green South Pacific sometimes used large money. They even drilled a hole into a 12-foot, very heavy stone and used it as a coin. Two men would insert a pole into the huge coin and carry it to the village of the person being paid. The earliest money in ancient times probably was salt. It was light, and traders could carry it easily over many, long and difficult miles.

GRAMMAR

▶ Fact and Opinion

WRITER'S CRAFT

Facts are true. **Opinions** are what someone thinks or feels. Writers can have the characters in their stories give opinions. This adds interest and helps readers understand why characters act the way they do.

Read the following story. On the lines, write opinions for the characters to give.

There were lots of things for a family to see and do at Mount Rushmore. Besides the mountain itself, there was a gift shop, movie, video clips, and many other exhibits. Cody laughed as he watched Teddy Roosevelt smile in a video clip of a toothpaste commercial.

Emily was the first to notice the screen with different pictures showing the construction of the presidents' faces. In front of the screen was a dynamite plunger. Emily touched a picture on the screen, pushed the plunger, and watched dynamite sculpt Abraham Lincoln's face. "_____."

Emily called to her mom and brother, Cody.

Later that evening, their mother asked them what they thought was the best thing about their visit to Mount Rushmore. Cody said,

"_____."

But Emily said, "_____

_____."

Fact and Opinion • Challenge

▶Cause and Effect

Alexander's grandparents gave him one dollar and for various reasons, Alexander lost all of his money. For example, he saw a bargain and thought he had to spend money. He called his brother a name and he had to pay his father. Both of these events, in addition to others, were causes that led to Alexander losing all of his money.

Alexander is getting another chance. His grandparents have sent him a dollar for his birthday. What will Alexander do with it? Will he be able to save it, like he wanted to do with the first dollar? Or will there be more garage sales or another sweet treat? Will he be able to control his temper when his brothers tease him?

Write two paragraphs about what happens when Alexander receives his birthday money. Be sure to include sentences that use clue words to signal cause-and-effect relationships. If you need more room, continue writing on another piece of paper.

_____

_____

_____

_____

_____

_____

_____

COMPREHENSION

UNIT 4 Money • **Lesson 2** *Alexander, Who Used to Be Rich Last Sunday*

▶Final Double Consonants

SPELLING

Rhyming Word Strategy
Write three words that rhyme with each word below and have the same spelling pattern.

1. smell _____

2. fall _____

3. mess _____

4. spill _____

Meaning Strategy
Write a sentence using each of the words below.

1. gull _____

2. till _____

3. guess _____

4. mitt _____

5. odd _____

UNIT 4 Money • **Lesson 2** *Alexander, Who Used to Be Rich Last Sunday*

▶The Suffix *-ly*

▶Replace each underlined word with the same word ending in *-ly*. Write the word on the line.

1. The puppy barked <u>playful</u>. _____

2. Dennis talked <u>quick</u>. _____

3. Dad drives <u>careful</u>. _____

4. She sings <u>beautiful</u>. _____

5. He <u>happy</u> agreed to help us move. _____

6. She <u>skillful</u> operated on the patient. _____

▶Write two sentences using describing words ending in *-ly*.

1. _____

2. _____

VOCABULARY

UNIT 4 Money • **Lesson 2** *Alexander, Who Used to Be Rich Last Sunday*

▶ Subjects and Predicates

The **subject** of a sentence names who or what the sentence is about; the **predicate** tells what the subject is or does.

▶ **Underline the complete subject and circle the predicate in these sentences.**

1. Inflation causes prices to rise.

2. The recession of the early 70s was hard on many families.

3. The members of the Federal Reserve set interest rates.

4. The word *interest* means the extra money that is made on a loan or deposit.

5. The Federal Reserve also strongly controls the nation's money supply.

6. The elderly, compassionate Dr. Frances Townsend helped start Social Security.

▶ **Some subjects and predicates are unusual, sometimes they are in a different order, and sometimes the subject is not even written. Underline the subject and circle the predicate in these sentences.**

7. Who stole my money?

8. Why do you think it was stolen?

9. Where is it?

10. How do you think it was stolen?

11. Is this your money?

Subjects and Predicates • Challenge

GRAMMAR

UNIT 4 Money • **Lesson 2** *Alexander, Who Used to Be Rich Last Sunday*

 # Time and Order Words

Time and **order** words show when and in what order events happen. These words help organize your writing and make it easier to follow.

▶ **Read the following information taken from the *Scholastic Book of World Records on* The World's Greatest Annual Snowfall.**

1,224 inches Mount Rainier, Washington   between 1971 and 1972

1,122 inches Paradise Station, Washington   between 1971 and 1972

▶ **Next, read this information from *The World Almanac for Kids 2000.* Hottest Places in the U.S.**

| California | 134 degrees F | 1913 |
| Arizona | 128 degrees F | 1994 |

▶ **Finally, write a paragraph about snowfall, temperature, or other weather topic. Use the information above, or look up facts about the weather in books, magazines, encyclopedias, or on the Internet web site www.weather.com. Be sure to use time and order words to keep track of the time and order of weather events.**

_____

_____

_____

_____

WRITER'S CRAFT

UNIT 4 Money • **Lesson 3** *Kids Did It! in Business*

►Contractions

Proofreading Strategy
Circle the misspelled contraction in each sentence.
Then write the contractions correctly on the lines.

1. Maybe sh'ell win first prize. _____

2. Weed like to go to the concert too. _____

3. We think its the best show ever! _____

4. Youl have to meet us there. _____

5. Do you think they'l be late? _____

Visualization Strategy
Circle the correct spelling for each contraction. Then
write it on the line.

1. whats   what's   what'z   _____

2. well   wheel   we'll   _____

3. youd   you'd   u'd   _____

4. can't   cant   can'd   _____

5. Id   eyed   I'd   _____

SPELLING

Name _____ Date _____

 # Business Vocabulary

Fill in the blank with a technology word from the box that best completes each sentence.

disk	save	contract	Internet	password	print

1. Did you sign a _____ for the work you completed?

2. I can't remember my _____ to log onto my computer.

3. Make sure to _____ your work or you might lose it.

4. You can go to the _____ and look for information.

5. _____ your paper and proofread it.

6. Save your work to a _____ and hand it in.

VOCABULARY

UNIT 4 Money • **Lesson 3** *Kids Did It! in Business*

►Parentheses and Periods

Many abbreviations, all abbreviations of titles, and all initials of people take a period. Use parentheses to set off information that is not essential to the meaning of the sentence.

►**Some of these sentences take parentheses and some do not. Put parentheses around extra information that is not essential to the meaning of the sentence.**

1. Bill Clinton was our first president from Arkansas.

2. Bill Clinton from Arkansas was our 42nd president.

3. She signed up for four years in the navy two on land and two at sea.

►**Change into abbreviations the words with lines to their right.**

4. Doctor _____ Albright's Meaty Chili

5. January _____ 3rd is my birthday.

6. Can you go on Wednesday _____ ?

►**Add periods where needed.**

7. Mrs Finley loves salad.

8. Dr Jenkins and Mr Hanson play golf.

9. He is an atty for the state

Name _____ Date _____

 # Structure of a Business Letter

A business letter that has a good structure makes a good impression and is more likely to get results. A business letter contains six parts: **heading, inside address, greeting, body, closing,** and **signature.**

Make a list of ideas for writing business letters. Perhaps you have a complaint about a book you have ordered. Would you like the park service to send you information about field trip adventures? Choose a topic and write a draft of a business letter. Be sure to use all six parts of a business letter. Then make a clean, corrected copy of your letter. Finally address an envelope and put a stamp on it. Now you are ready to mail your business letter.

_____

_____

_____

_____

_____

_____

_____

_____

_____

_____

WRITER'S CRAFT

UNIT 4 Money • **Lesson 4** *The Cobbler's Song*

COMPREHENSION

▶ Author's Purpose

Be Informed!

The author's purpose for writing "The Cobbler's Song" was to entertain the reader. Some selections are written mainly to inform. How do the two types of text differ? Try your hand at one.

News reporters write to inform readers of current happenings or even longer investigations of events. Imagine you are a news reporter for your school. Write an article to inform the other students. Here are some questions to give you some ideas. Has there been a recent art or science fair? Is there a problem you have noticed? Is there an upcoming assembly or school concert? Did one of your classmates do something very special? Is there a project your class or even the whole school could do together? Remember to give your news article a title.

Title

_____

_____

_____

_____

_____

_____

_____

_____

_____

UNIT 4 Money • **Lesson 4** *The Cobbler's Song*

▶Adding -ed and -ing

Conventions Strategy
Add *-ing* to each word. Then write a sentence using each new word to show something that is happening now. Remember to drop the final *e*.

1. hike _____ _____

2. shake _____ _____

3. bite _____ _____

4. hide _____ _____

5. dive _____ _____

Meaning Strategy
Fill in each blank with a word from the box that best completes each sentence.

entered	skated	prized	opened

1. When she _____ the box, a puppy jumped out!

2. We _____ the house through the garage when we lost our keys.

3. She brushed her _____ horse every day.

4. We _____ on the pond last winter.

SPELLING

UNIT 4 Money • **Lesson 4** *The Cobbler's Song*

▶The Endings *-ed* and *-ing*

VOCABULARY

▶**Follow the directions for each number below. Be sure to use words with *-ed* or *-ing*.**

1. Write a sentence that describes something you did yesterday.

_____

2. Write a sentence telling what you are doing now.

_____

3. Write a sentence that describes something you did last summer.

_____

4. Write a sentence describing what you would rather be doing now.

_____

▶**Use each word below in a sentence.**

1. drawing _____

2. played _____

3. swimming _____

Name _____ Date _____

▶Pronouns

Possessive pronouns express ownership. It is important to know the difference between personal and possessive pronouns.

▶ **Circle the possessive pronouns and underline the personal pronouns in these sentences.**

In 1781, Robert Morris started the Bank of North America with his own money. It helped get loans to fight the British. Its reserves were also used to pay the Revolutionary War debt. In 1791 Alexander Hamilton started the first Bank of the United States. He was Secretary of the Treasury, and his idea was to help control prices and the money supply.

▶ **Rewrite these sentences so that the possessive pronoun stands alone after the verb.**

1. That is your bike.

_____

2. That is my dollar.

_____

3. These are her books.

_____

4. That is their home.

_____

WRITER'S CRAFT

▶ Avoiding Wordiness

Wordiness makes writing unclear and may cause readers to misunderstand and lose interest.

▶ **Read the following paragraph. On the lines below rewrite the paragraph to avoid wordiness and make the paragraph more understandable.**

    An object or thing that orbits in a circle around a planet is known to be called a satellite. A moon is a natural, not manmade, satellite. Manmade satellites are constructed by people. They are used for the purposes of taking photographic pictures of our own planet Earth and for TV, cell phone, and all types of communication signals. These kinds of satellites are also used for the purpose of space stations and as observatories where people can gather information about the planets, stars, and all things about astronomy.

_____

_____

_____

_____

_____

_____

_____

_____

▶Adding -s or -es

Visualization Strategy
Circle the correct spelling for each word. Then write it on the line.

1. sleevies   sleevs   sleeves   _____

2. horsies   hors's   horses   _____

3. guppies   guppys   guppes   _____

4. babys   babies   babyes   _____

5. donkees   donkies   donkeys   _____

Meaning Strategy
Write each word from the box next to its meaning.

britches	bunnies	pennies	hobbies	berries

1. small fruit   _____

2. baby rabbits   _____

3. fun activities   _____

4. pants   _____

5. coins   _____

SPELLING

Name _____ Date _____

▶ Compound Words

VOCABULARY

▶ Take off the second word in each compound word below. Then add a word of your own to the first word to make a new compound word. Write the new compound word on the line.

Example:

    anyone   anything, anywhere, anyhow, anybody

1. fireplace _____

2. infield _____

3. snowplow _____

4. something _____

5. windsurfing _____

▶ Make compound words from the words in the box and use them in a sentence.

day	class	sun	any	birth	light	one	mate

1. _____

2. _____

3. _____

4. _____

▶Subject/Verb Agreement

Verbs and subjects should agree in number: singular subjects take singular verbs, and plural subjects take plural verbs.

▶**For each of these sentences, circle the verb that agrees in number.**

1. The team eats/eat at the same restaurant before every game.

2. The teammates eats/eat at the same restaurant before every game.

3. One-half of the class are/is going to the cafeteria.

4. The group are/is going to the museum this afternoon.

5. Many members of the group are/is going to the museum this afternoon.

6. The jurors was/were late returning from lunch.

7. The jury was/were late returning from lunch.

8. Politics is/are her real interest.

9. Linguistics are/is the study of language.

10. *Of Mice and Men* was/were written by John Steinbeck.

11. The number of voters have/has declined.

12. A number of voters has/have not voted this election.

UNIT 4 Money • **Lesson 5** *Four Dollars and Fifty Cents*

Sentence Combining

Sentence combining adds variety and interest to your writing.

Read the following postcard. Help make the postcard more interesting by combining short choppy sentences with conjunctions. Rewrite the postcard on the lines below, using commas before conjunctions.

Dear Grandma,

   I went to the zoo on Saturday. I saw some very strange animals.The world's largest spider is a Goliath birdeater. It is commonly known as a giant tarantula. It is called a birdeater. It really eats insects and small reptiles. It was 11 inches long. It was very hairy. I'm glad it was in a glass cage!

                                    Love,

                                    Amy

_____

_____

_____

_____

_____

_____

_____

Sentence Combining • Challenge

▶ Sequence

What is the Right Order?

Unscramble each group of words and write them in the correct order to make a sentence. Remember to begin with a capital letter and end with a period. Then, write the numbers *1* through *6* in the boxes beside the sentences to tell the correct order of the events in the story.

☐ her then nest her was all in she when laid eggs it done _____

_____

☐ searched the perfect bluebird over all nest for the place mother

to build a _____

_____

☐ lived the who safe in house with the people the saw the nest and

porch kept it _____

_____

☐ nest leaves she went out then twigs and build her collecting to

_____

_____

☐ spent nest a long she her building time _____

_____

☐ looking perfect all she roof under found the day spot a porch after

_____

_____

UNIT 4 Money • **Lesson 6** *The Go-Around Dollar*

►Compound Words

Compound Word Strategy
Use a word from the box to spell a new compound word with the underlined word below. Write the new word on the line.

tie	hog	way	place	walk

1. play<u>ground</u>   _____

2. chalk<u>board</u>   _____

3. side<u>walk</u>   _____

4. rain<u>bow</u>   _____

5. camp<u>fire</u>   _____

Meaning Word Strategy
Make up two more compound words and use them each in a sentence.

1. _____

2. _____

Compound Words • Challenge

SPELLING

UNIT 4 Money • **Lesson 6** *The Go-Around Dollar*

▶Money Words

Fill in the blank with a money word from the box that best completes each sentence.

change	quarter	cash	dollars	cost	bills

1. How much _____ will that game cost me?

2. If you put a _____ into the machine, you can get a gumball.

3. How much _____ will I get if I give you ten dollars?

4. I don't have any coins, I just have _____.

5. Will fifty _____ be enough?

6. How much does this baseball card _____?

VOCABULARY

▶ Comparative and Superlative Adverbs

GRAMMAR

Comparative adverbs compare two actions; **superlative adverbs** compare three or more actions.

▶ **After each sentence, write *comparative* or *superlative*.**

1. Brendan invests the smartest. _____

2. Yolanda saves more wisely than Brian. _____

3. This store marks prices higher than that store.

   _____

4. The line at this bank moves the most slowly.

   _____

5. That bank gives loans more easily. _____

▶ **Some comparative and superlative adverbs are irregular. What are the comparative and superlative of these two adverbs?**

Well: _____

Badly: _____

▶Supporting Details

Supporting details are facts, examples, and reasons that give readers more information and understanding about your main idea.

Think about the sports or games you like to watch and play. Now use some of the things you like about those sports and games to invent a new game.

Give your game a name and decide on the details of your game. How many players will be on each team? What kind of ball or other equipment will be used? How will your game be played?

Then write a paragraph on another piece of paper about the game you have invented. Include all the supporting details that help explain your game.

Plan your Game

Name of Your Game: _____

Number of Players: _____

Equipment Needed: _____

_____

Rules of the Game: _____

_____

_____

_____

WRITER'S CRAFT

UNIT 4 Money • **Lesson 7** *Uncle Jed's Barbershop*

▶Unit 4 Review

Visualization Strategy
Circle the correct spelling for each word. Then write it on the line.

SPELLING

1. is'nt   isn't   isnt   _____

2. stitches   stitchies   stitchs   _____

3. monkys   monkies   monkeys   _____

4. winer   winner   winnor   _____

5. saveing   saving   savving   _____

Rhyming Word Strategy
Write two words that rhyme with each word below.

1. will _____

2. taking _____

3. died _____

4. clippers _____

▶Unit 4 Review

Follow the directions for each number below.

1. Write a sentence using a word ending in *-ly*.

_____

2. Write a sentence using a word ending in *-ed*.

_____

3. Write a sentence using a word ending in *-ing*.

_____

4. Write a sentence using a compound word.

_____

5. Write two words in the base word family for the word *understand*.

_____

VOCABULARY

▶Review

GRAMMAR

▶**Circle the possessive pronoun that agrees in number with its antecedent.**

1. Everyone has (their/his or her) own way of spending money.

2. People have (his or her/their) own way of spending money.

▶**Circle the subject and underline the predicate.**

1. Who wrote that song?

2. When were you going to tell me?

3. Would you help me move these boxes?

4. How are you?

▶**Explain in one sentence what a preposition does. Then give two examples of each function.**

_____

_____

▶**Circle the verb that agrees with the pronoun.**

5. She (study/studies/studys) every night.

6. I (study/studies/studys) less than she does.

7. You (study/studies/studys) a lot too.

8. He (study/studies/studys) most of all.

9. We (study/studies/studys) together sometimes.

UNIT 4 Money • **Lesson 7** *Uncle Jed's Barbershop*

▶ Effective Beginnings and Endings

WRITER'S CRAFT

Effective beginnings grab and hold the reader's attention. **Effective endings** sum up and keep readers thinking about the subject. Remember your audience and purpose whenever you write.

Pick a president you admire. Use the dictionary, encyclopedia, books, or Internet to find information about this president.

Next, write a paragraph about the president you chose. Use an interesting or surprising fact to begin your paragraph. Include new information you found about the president in your paragraph. Write an effective ending that sums up what you learned about this president.

_____

_____

_____

_____

_____

_____

_____

_____

_____

_____

UNIT 5 Storytelling • **Lesson I** *A Story, A Story*

COMPREHENSION

▶ Sequence

Unscramble each group of words and write them in the correct order to make a sentence. Remember to begin with a capital letter and end with a period. Then, write the numbers *1* through *5* in the boxes beside the sentences to tell the correct order of the events in the story.

huckleberry   came   a   soon   to   bush   it

☐ _____

_____

bear   cave   morning   one   left   a   cub   its

☐ _____

_____

cave   the   back   its   hurried   after   its   cub   snack   to

☐ _____

_____

and   berries   cub   all   the   ripe   down   nibbled   sat   the

☐ _____

_____

along   wooded   path   walking   it   started   a   narrow

☐ _____

_____

▶Consonant Blends: *spl-, str-,* and *spr-*

 Consonant-Substitution Strategy Add *spl, str,* or *spr* to each word ending to make words. Write the word or words on the line.

1. ing   _____

2. int   _____

3. ap   _____

4. ain   _____

 Meaning Strategy Fill in the blank with a word from the box that best completes each sentence.

splatter	sprinkle	sticky	sprout	stronger

1. _____ the plants with water.

2. Our hands were _____ with cotton candy.

3. Lifting weights made her _____ .

4. Soon the seeds will _____ into plants.

5. The car made the muddy water _____ against the house.

UNIT 5 Storytelling • **Lesson I** *A Story, A Story*

▶ Levels of Specificity

Put some words about food in the correct categories.

                              ┌─── Food ───┐
                        Fruits   Vegetables   Meats

Example: apple   broccoli   turkey

_____   _____   _____

_____   _____   _____

_____   _____   _____

VOCABULARY

UNIT 5 Storytelling • **Lesson I** *A Story, A Story*

 # Sentence Structure

Three of the most common ways to join simple sentences are with the conjunctions *and*, *but*, and *or*. When these join sentences, put a comma in front of them.

▶ **Join each of these pairs of simple sentences about Greek mythology with the appropriate conjunction.**

1. Artemis and Apollo are twins. They are the children of Hera and Zeus.

   _____

   _____

2. Artemis may be called *Diana*. She may be called *Cynthia*.

   _____

   _____

3. Apollo is god of the sun. He is not the god of the moon.

   _____

▶ **Break these compound sentences down into their simple sentences.**

4. Hermes is the son of Zeus, but Hestia is Zeus' sister.

   _____

5. Demeter is Zeus' sister, and she is the sister of Hestia.

   _____

MECHANICS

UNIT 5 Storytelling • **Lesson I** *A Story, A Story*

▶Organization of Narrative Writing

WRITER'S CRAFT

Good **organization of narrative writing** makes your story easy for readers to read and follow the sequence of events.

Choose an event to write about in a narration. It can be something that has happened to you, a relative, a friend, or an exciting event from your own imagination. Maybe something funny happened at a birthday party.

Use the numbered lines to organize your narration. Read over your story plan to check that the organization makes sense. Then write out your narration on a separate piece of paper. Be sure to give your story a title.

Beginning: _____

_____

Middle: **1.** _____

2. _____

3. _____

Ending: _____

_____

▶Setting

The **setting** is the time and place that the events of a story happen. The characters can give clues about the setting. Good writers let their readers know when the setting changes.

Read the following story. Then think about an ending for the story that happens in a different time and place. On the lines below, write an ending that includes a setting change.

Hannah and David waited patiently for their turn to ride the Ferris Wheel. Moments later they were stopped at the top, looking down at the rides, games, and their tiny mom. All too soon the ride was over.

"One more ride, and then we go." said Mom.

"Let's go to the fun house," David suggested.

They laughed as they tried to walk on the moving floors, and through the rolling tubes.

The family was tired but happy as they headed for the parking lot. "What could top an evening like this?" David thought to himself.

_____

_____

_____

_____

_____

WRITER'S CRAFT

UNIT 5 Storytelling • **Lesson 2** *Oral History*

▶ Silent *k* and *w*

Visualization Strategy Circle the correct spelling for each word. Then write it on the line.

1. ryte   write   wriet   _____

2. nee   knei   knee   _____

3. riten   ritten   written   _____

4. knit   knet   nit   _____

5. wrek   wreck   reck   _____

Meaning Strategy Fill in each blank with a word from the box that best completes each sentence.

knew	knife	wrap	wrong

1. Can you help me _____ her birthday gift?

2. I _____ all the answers to the questions.

3. We went the _____ way.

4. Use a _____ to cut the apple.

SPELLING

Name _____ Date _____

 # Homographs

Write two sentences using each word. Be sure to use a
different meaning for the word in each sentence.

1. close _____

_____

2. minute _____

_____

3. object _____

_____

4. present _____

_____

5. sow _____

_____

6. wind _____

_____

VOCABULARY

Name ________________________________ Date __________

MECHANICS

Colons

Colons come before a list when there is a complete thought before the list. Add colons and commas to these sentences as needed. Only those with complete thoughts before the list will take a colon.

1. The most powerful gods and goddesses of ancient Greece were Zeus Hera and Poseidon.
2. Zeus had a number of children who also were Greek deities Athena Apollo Artemis Ares Hephaestus and Hermes.
3. Zeus also had a sister named Hestia a sister named Demeter and a brother named Poseidon.
4. One day three Greek gods and goddesses were arguing Zeus Hera and Leto.
5. Hera had some things to say to Zeus banish Leto from Mt. Olympus never see her again and do not bring her back.
6. Apollo was the god of poetry music medicine and light.
7. Other gods and goddesses took care of other things fire invention agriculture war love marriage and the ocean for example.
8. There were three less powerful gods Pan Hades and Dionysus.

Name _____ Date _____

▶Telling in Time Order

Telling in time order is using time words to keep track of the order of events in a story or report.

If you could plan the perfect weekend what would you do? On the lines below, list the things you would want to do for your perfect weekend. Then number the items on your list in the order you would do them.

_____

_____

_____

_____

Next, think about what time your weekend would begin. When would you eat? What would you do Saturday afternoon? When would you go to bed?

Now, write about your perfect weekend. Be sure to use time words to tell in time order everything you would want to do.

_____

_____

_____

_____

_____

WRITER'S CRAFT

UNIT 5 Storytelling • **Lesson 3** *Storm in the Night*

▶Author's Purpose

An author's purpose can be to entertain, inform, explain, or persuade the reader. "Storm in the Night" was written primarily to entertain.

▶**Write two sentences to explain why Grandfather felt afraid.**

_____

_____

_____

_____

▶**Write two sentences to persuade others to record their family history.**

_____

_____

_____

_____

▶**Write three or four sentences to inform others about thunderstorms. You may use an encyclopedia, a book from the school library, or the Internet to find information.**

_____

_____

_____

_____

UNIT 5 Storytelling • **Lesson 3** *Storm in the Night*

▶Words with *-lf, -mb,* and *-tch*

 Rhyming Strategy Write two words that rhyme with each word below.

1. match _____

2. ditch _____

3. thumb _____

 Visualization Strategy Write the correct spelling for each word. Then use each word in a sentence of your own.

1. com _____

_____

2. lam _____

_____

3. clim _____

_____

4. caf _____

_____

5. lim _____

_____

SPELLING

UNIT 5 Storytelling • **Lesson 3** *Storm in the Night*

►Suffixes

Add the suffix *-ly* or *-ness* to each underlined word. Write the new words on the lines.

1. The <u>dark</u> of the sky told us a storm was coming. _____

2. He <u>slow</u> crept up on the frightened bird. _____

3. She <u>clever</u> figured out the mystery. _____

4. His <u>sick</u> lasted two weeks. _____

5. The music was playing <u>loud</u>. _____

6. Her <u>calm</u> made us all feel better. _____

VOCABULARY

▶Conjunctions and Interjections

And, *but*, and *or* are conjunctions that join words or groups of words. Interjections are expressions of strong emotion that are followed by an exclamation point.

In the line at the end of the sentence, write the interjection that expresses the emotion of the sentence. Use *Ouch!*, *Wow!*, *Oops!*, *Whew!*, *Hey!*, and *Aha!*

1. It hurts when I hit my thumb with a hammer. _____

2. I dropped my books. _____

3. I caught you now with your hand in the cookie jar. _____

4. I almost fell on the ice, but I caught myself just in time. _____

5. That sunset is beautiful. _____

6. Give me back my marbles. _____

Pretend you are the teacher, and you need to explain the conjunctions *and*, *but*, and *or* to the class. All of them connect words, but they connect words differently. Write one sentence to explain how *and* connects words, one sentence to explain how *but* connects words, and one sentence to explain how *or* connects words.

_____

_____

_____

MECHANICS

UNIT 5   Storytelling • **Lesson 3** *Storm in the Night*

▶Exact Words

WRITER'S CRAFT

Exact words help readers imagine the same picture the writer imagines. Writers can choose exact words from their own vocabularies. Writers can also find choices in a thesaurus or dictionary.

▶For each word below, write two exact words. Use a dictionary or thesaurus if you need to find more exact words.

road _____

go _____

think _____

friend _____

write _____

ask _____

▶Now, write a paragraph using six of the exact words that you found.

_____

_____

_____

_____

_____

_____

UNIT 5 Storytelling • **Lesson 4** *Carving the Pole*

▶The /ə/ Sound

Visualization Strategy Circle the correct spelling for each word. Then write it on the line.

1. legind   legond   legend   _____

2. womin   woman   womun   _____

3. systim   systam   system   _____

4. lisen   listen   listin   _____

5. horizon   horizen   horizin   _____

Proofreading Strategy Circle the misspelled word in each sentence. Then write the correct spelling on the line.

1. It is easier to divide evin numbers. _____

2. Mom grows carrots and lettuce in her gardin. _____

3. The lessen today will be on mammals. _____

4. How did this get brokon? _____

5. The robon sang a sweet song. _____

SPELLING

Name _____ Date _____

▶Cultural Words

VOCABULARY

Choose a cultural word from the box that will best complete each sentence.

skunk	tepees	brave	moccasins	canoe

1. Some Native Americans lived in cone-shaped houses called

   _____.

2. A _____ is an Indian warrior.

3. Many people use a _____ to cross a river.

4. _____ are soft, flat shoes made of leather.

5. A _____ will spray an enemy with a bad odor to protect itself.

UNIT 5   Storytelling • **Lesson 4** *Carving the Pole*

▶Capitalization and Underlining

Greetings and closing of letters, direct quotes, titles of media, and titles of written works should be capitalized.

Titles of books, magazines, newspapers, TV shows, movies, and plays should be underlined.

▶ **Circle any letters that should be capitalized.**

1. Hera said to Leto, "you must leave Mt. Olympus."

2. dear Cindy,

3. I read an article called "bubbles."

▶ **Indicate which titles below should be underlined.**

4. My father uses The Joy of Cooking when he makes dinner.

5. Her favorite magazine is Harper's.

6. My little brother likes to watch The Elephant Show.

7. We rented the movie Romeo and Juliet.

WRITER'S CRAFT

▶ Sentence Elaboration and Expansion

Good writers *elaborate and expand sentences* by adding extra information about their subject.

Read the information about bamboo. Use the information to write a paragraph about this plant. Elaborate and expand your sentences by using parentheses and prepositional phrases to add extra information. Use a comma and a conjunction to combine short sentences.

Give your paragraph a title and write it out on the lines below.

Facts about Bamboo: world's fastest growing land plant
grows 1 foot a day
can grow to 130 feet
grows in tropical and subtropical climates
most of world's bamboo is in
        east and southeast parts of Asia
is a type of grass

_____

_____

_____

_____

_____

_____

_____

UNIT 5 Storytelling • **Lesson 5** *The Keeping Quilt*

▶Fact and Opinion

▶**Read each sentence. Circle the letter under the appropriate column: Fact or Opinion.**

		Fact	Opinion
1.	Riding a bus is fun.	w	k
2.	Grandpa picks Jenny up from school every day.	e	a
3.	They are building a new store on that lot.	e	t
4.	Hot summer days are great!	e	p
5.	There was a traffic jam at the bridge.	i	r
6.	Old buildings are interesting.	m	n
7.	Plants are found in empty lots.	g	e
8.	Streets in a city are paved.	q	l
9.	People in a city can ride buses or subways.	u	o
10.	People living in a city are happy.	n	i
11.	You can check books out at the library.	l	z
12.	My favorite books are about mysteries.	b	t

COMPREHENSION

▶**Now, write the letters you circled to make the word that answers this riddle.**

I'm warm, soft, and animals prance across my top. Sometimes I am seen high overhead at a wedding.

I am a _____.

UNIT 5 Storytelling • **Lesson 5** *The Keeping Quilt*

▶ The /kw/ and /skw/ Sounds

SPELLING

Visualization Strategy Write the correct spelling for each word. Then use each word in a sentence of your own.

1. skwirrel _____

_____

2. qwick _____

_____

3. skwint _____

_____

4. qwestion _____

_____

5. qwiet _____

_____

Proofreading Strategy Circle the misspelled word in each sentence. Then write the words correctly on the lines.

1. Did you hear a mouse sweak? _____

2. I heard a duck qwack. _____

3. Don't skwirt your eye with that lemon. _____

4. Be qwiet during the movie. _____

UNIT 5 Storytelling • **Lesson 5** *The Keeping Quilt*

▶ Words with Foreign Origins

Write the foreign word from the box that matches each definition.

ranch	pasta	yarn	cotton	pajamas	boulevard

1. A kind of noodle _____

2. A large farm _____

3. Clothes worn to bed _____

4. Thread used in knitting _____

5. A street _____

6. Soft, fluffy fiber _____

VOCABULARY

▶Capitalization

MECHANICS

Do research in the classroom library to answer
the following questions. Be sure to use the correct
capitalization.

1. What language is spoken in Trinidad? _____

2. What is the name of the largest river in Brazil? _____

3. What language is spoken in Peru? _____

4. What ocean does Vietnam lie along? _____

5. What river is Paris, France, on? _____

6. What ocean does Liberia lie along? _____

7. What is the capital of Cuba? _____

8. What is the main language of the Ivory Coast? _____

9. What river is New York City on? _____

10. What language is spoken in Moldova? _____

11. What is the capital of China? _____

12. What is the name of the largest art museum in Paris? _____

13. Who designed the glass pyramid outside the entrance to it?

    _____

Suspense and Surprise

Including suspense and surprise in your stories can make your writing more interesting.

Think of a confusing or mysterious problem that your character will have to find an answer for or solve. Then think of 2 different possible solutions for your problem. Plan information that will lead your character (and your audience) toward each solution. Save the best information for the surprise at the end.

Write your story on the lines below. Build suspense by adding sounds and telling how the character is feeling.

_____

_____

_____

_____

_____

_____

_____

_____

_____

WRITER'S CRAFT

UNIT 5 Storytelling • **Lesson 6** *Johnny Appleseed*

▶The /s/ and /j/ Sounds

 Rhyming Strategy Write three words that rhyme with each word below.

1. nice _____

2. sink _____

3. age _____

 Visualization Strategy Circle the correct spelling for each word. Then write it on the line.

1. suace   sauce   sause   _____

2. gim   jym   gym   _____

3. cellar   celler   sellar   _____

4. cince   sinse   since   _____

5. gurm   germ   jerm   _____

6. megic   majic   magic   _____

UNIT 5 Storytelling • **Lesson 6** *Johnny Appleseed*

▶ Prefixes

Add the prefix *re-* or *un-* to each word to make a new word. Write a sentence using each word.

1. clean _____

_____

2. eaten _____

_____

3. afraid _____

_____

4. play _____

_____

5. alike _____

_____

6. tell _____

_____

7. start _____

_____

8. hurt _____

_____

VOCABULARY

UNIT 5 Storytelling • **Lesson 6** *Johnny Appleseed*

▶Capitalization

MECHANICS

▶**Fill in the answers to the following questions using the correct capitalization.**

1. What month is named after the Roman god Janus?

   _____

2. What day is named for the sun? _____

3. What day of the week is named for the Roman god Saturn?

   _____

4. What month is named after the Roman emperor Julius Caesar?

   _____

5. What day of the week is named for the moon? _____

6. What month is named after the Roman emperor Caesar

   Augustus? _____

▶**Circle the letters that should be capitalized in this paragraph about special events and their related historical periods.**

   The great crash started the great depression.

The constitutional convention was an important

event during the colonial period. The chicago

exposition celebrated the industrial revolution.

Annual reenactments of the battle of gettysburg

help us remember the civil war.

Capitalization • Challenge

Dialogue

Dialogue is the conversation between two or more characters in a story. Dialogue makes the characters seem more real, and helps to move the story along.

Read the following riddle. Then rewrite the riddle as if you were telling it to someone who doesn't get the right answer. (Many people think the answer is 15 minutes.) Be sure to use speaker tags and quotation marks.

There are two bugs in a jar, a male and a female. They multiply very fast. In fact, they double their number every minute. The jar is completely full of bugs in half an hour. When is the jar half full of bugs? Twenty-nine minutes.

_____

_____

_____

_____

_____

_____

_____

_____

_____

WRITER'S CRAFT

WRITER'S CRAFT

▶Exaggeration

Exaggeration is describing something in a way that stretches the truth. Exaggeration makes people and events larger than life.

First pick a physical skill that you have or would like to have. Next, take this skill to the limits of your imagination. Maybe you run so fast, you run on top of water. Make your exaggeration as outrageous as you want.

On the lines below, write a paragraph about yourself and your incredible accomplishment. Don't forget to give yourself a great title.

_____

_____

_____

_____

_____

_____

_____

_____

_____

_____

▶ Author's Point of View

▶ A Different Point of View

"Aunt Flossie's Hats (and Crab Cakes Later)" was written from the first-person point of view. Imagine you are reporting on the story and writing it down for others to read. How will you describe the action? Will you tell it matter-of-factly, like a news story? Or will you tell it with lots of descriptive details, like an entertaining fictional story? How you tell it is up to you, but experiment with writing from the third-person point of view.

_____

_____

_____

_____

_____

_____

_____

_____

_____

_____

_____

_____

COMPREHENSION

UNIT 5 Storytelling • **Lesson 7** *Aunt Flossie's Hats (and Crab Cakes Later)*

▶ Unit 5 Review

 Rhyming Strategy Replace the underlined word in each sentence with a rhyming word from the box.

quake	wrote	racing	city	spray

1. I like to watch horse <u>facing</u>. _____

2. In what <u>pity</u> do you live? _____

3. My friend <u>tote</u> a short story for school. _____

4. <u>Play</u> the car before you wash it. _____

5. I saw him <u>shake</u> with fear. _____

 Visualization Strategy Write the correct spelling for each word. Then use each word in a sentence of your own.

1. buttens _____

_____

2. plunje _____

_____

3. sevin _____

_____

4. enjines _____

_____

SPELLING

Name _____ Date _____

▶Unit 5 Review

▶Write a sentence with a word of your own for each prefix or suffix below.

1. re- _____

2. un- _____

3. -ly _____

4. -ness _____

▶Write both definitions for each homograph below.

1. bow _____

2. wound _____

3. compact _____

4. live _____

5. record _____

VOCABULARY

MECHANICS

▶Review

▶**Add colons, capitalize, underline, and punctuate as needed.**

Have you seen the movie an american quilt? I own a quilt made by four family members my great-grandmother, her aunt, her sister, and her daughter. It tells the story of when they came to America. I read about quilts in a book called with needle and thread. Then I found out the names of three quilting magazines american patchwork and quilting, quilting today, and threads.

▶**Use a conjunction to join the sentences.**

1. This blue quilt was made in Laos. This blue quilt was made in West Virginia.

   _____

   _____

2. Patchwork is one way to make a quilt. Appliqué is another way to make a quilt.

   _____

   _____

Name _____ Date _____

▶ Plot

The **plot** is made up of the events that happen in a story. A story map separates the parts of the plot. A story map also shows how a plot builds to a climax.

Think of a story that you have read recently, or one that you know well. Then fill out the story map below. Write about the character or characters and the problem they have to solve. Next, write the events that build to the high point or climax. Write what the climax of the story is, then write out how the story ends. Add or cross out lines as needed.

Title : _____

Character Description: _____

Character's Problem: _____

Event 1: _____

Event 2: _____

Event 3: _____

Climax or High Point: _____

Ending: _____

WRITER'S CRAFT

UNIT 6 Country Life • **Lesson I** *The Country Mouse and the City Mouse*

▶Irregular Plurals

Conventions Strategy
Write the plural form of each word on the line.

1. deer _____

2. wolf _____

3. sheep _____

4. mouse _____

5. wife _____

Proofreading Strategy
Circle the misspelled word in each sentence. Then spell the word correctly on the line.

1. I rake leafes for my neighbors in the fall. _____

2. Our mother cows had calfs last week. _____

3. The goozes swim on the pond in our backyard. _____

4. Our library has many shelfs of books. _____

5. My dad can eat many shrimpes for dinner. _____

Irregular Plurals • Challenge

UNIT 6 Country Life • **Lesson I** *The Country Mouse and the City Mouse*

▶Antonyms

▶Write a word that is an antonym for each
underlined word.

1. Did you <u>find</u> your cat? _____

2. I want to sit in the <u>back</u> seat! _____

3. Do you want to <u>sell</u> this clock? _____

4. Are you going to <u>leave</u>? _____

5. That movie was so <u>exciting</u>! _____

6. Be careful, the water is <u>shallow</u>. _____

▶Write three pairs of antonyms below.

1. _____

2. _____

3. _____

VOCABULARY

UNIT 6 Country Life • **Lesson I** *The Country Mouse and the City Mouse*

▶Commas

MECHANICS

▶*Yes* and *no* usually go at the beginning of the sentence, but they do not have to. Fill in the commas as needed.

1. Yes the economy of the South was based on cotton.

2. The economy of the South was based on cotton yes.

3. It was yes but now the economy is diverse.

4. Now the economy of the South is not based on cotton no.

5. No now the economy of the South is not based on cotton.

▶From this list match the cities and states, and write the pairs with commas: *Seattle, Miami, Texas, Florida, Washington,* and *Dallas.*

6. _____

7. _____

8. _____

▶Insert the commas that are missing in each sentence.

9. I just flew nine hours from Melbourne Australia to Los Angeles California the United States.

10. Rabat Morocco is in North Africa but Ottawa Canada is in North America.

Commas • Challenge

▶Effective Endings

An **effective ending** is one that sums up the subject and gives readers something more to think about. To make endings more effective, consider your audience and purpose when writing.

Read the story idea below. Now, write a final paragraph for the story. You can use humor or an interesting idea to help make your ending effective.

The King and Queen wanted to see for themselves how people lived outside the castle walls. This adventure was turning out to be much more than they had expected. The King had been arrested for telling people that he was the King. The Queen had been mistaken for a kitchen maid. She had spent the whole day crying, while she cut up onions for her own royal dinner party. No one would believe that they were really the King and Queen.

_____

_____

_____

_____

_____

_____

_____

WRITER'S CRAFT

UNIT 6 Country Life • **Lesson 2** *Heartland*

▶Fact and Opinion

COMPREHENSION

Good Enough to Eat

▶ **Many different crops are grown on farms. Think about your favorite food. Do you eat it raw? What crop or crops are used to make your favorite food? Choose one crop to learn more about. Use encyclopedias, magazines, library books, and the Internet to find out more about the crop. Write your notes on the lines below.**

_____

_____

_____

_____

▶ **Write a paragraph about the crop. Include facts and opinions in your sentence.**

_____

_____

_____

_____

_____

Fact and Opinion • Challenge

▶Double Consonants + y

Rhyming Word Strategy
Write the words from the box that rhyme with each word below.

foggy	funny	bunny	guppy	silly	soggy	chilly	sunny

1. runny _____

2. puppy _____

3. hilly _____

4. groggy _____

Visualization Strategy
Circle the correct spelling for each word. Then write it on the line.

1. sloopy   sloppy   slopee   _____

2. dizy   dizzey   dizzy   _____

3. grassey   grassy   grasy   _____

4. hilly   hillee   hilley   _____

5. smely   smelly   smelley   _____

SPELLING

Name _____ Date _____

▶Synonyms

VOCABULARY

Write a word that is a synonym for each word below. Then write a sentence using each word.

1. auto _____

_____

2. assist _____

_____

3. enjoy _____

_____

4. piece _____

_____

5. say _____

_____

6. attempt _____

_____

▶Apostrophes and Hyphens

▶**Put apostrophes in the correct position to form the possessive.**

Joint ownership and individual ownership: Form the possessive of the underlined words.

1. <u>Bert and Ernie</u> television show is called *Sesame Street.*

_____

_____

2. <u>Ford and Toyota</u> profits this year were higher than expected.

_____

_____

3. <u>General Motors and Honda</u> cars compete with each other for the same customers.

_____

_____

▶**Cross out unneeded apostrophes and add needed apostrophes.**

4. The Kuhns' farm is right next to our's.

5. Is the responsibility for milking Susans or your's?

6. Of all the animals, pigs are my favorite's.

7. Looks like we will have healthy crop's this year.

8. Is her's the brown or the palomino horse?

MECHANICS

WRITER'S CRAFT

▶Collecting and Organizing Data—Lists

Writers **collect and organize data in lists** to help them remember data, group related data, and to get ideas for writing.

Read the following information from *The World Almanac for Kids 2000*. Decide how you could organize the data into smaller, related lists. Create a heading for each list and organize the data into the smaller lists. When listing data, be sure to sum up information in your own words.

"**Temperate Forests.** Temperate forests have warm, rainy summers and cold, snowy winters. Here **deciduous trees** (which lose their leaves in the fall and grow new ones in the spring) join the evergreens. Temperate forests are home to maple, oak, beech, and poplar trees, and to wildflowers and shrubs. These forests are found in eastern United States, southeastern Canada, northern Europe and Asia, and southern Australia."

_____

_____

_____

_____

_____

_____

_____

▶Drawing Conclusions

▶ **Read each of the following paragraphs. Write a conclusion you can draw from each paragraph.**

Everyone in the class remembered all of their lines. Everyone remembered their cues. When we finished, the audience stood up and applauded.

Conclusion: _____

_____

A truck pulled up at the empty house next door. A new car was in the driveway. The men driving the truck started carrying furniture into the house.

Conclusion: _____

_____

▶ **Now, write a paragraph of your own from which a conclusion can be drawn. Then, trade papers with a partner and draw a conclusion from your partner's paragraph.**

_____

_____

_____

_____

_____

COMPREHENSION

UNIT 6 Country Life • **Lesson 3** *Leah's Pony*

▶ Words with -er and -est

SPELLING

Conventions Strategy
Add *-er* to each word. Then use it in a sentence that compares two things. Remember to double the final consonant and change the *y* to *i* in some words.

1. hungry _____

2. great _____

3. heavy _____

4. happy _____

Meaning Strategy
Fill in the blank with the word that best completes each sentence.

happiest	greatest	taller	prettier	heaviest

1. Who is _____, you or your sister?

2. When I won first prize, I was the _____ kid in the world!

3. My math book is the _____ book in my bag.

4. I think roses are _____ than tulips.

5. I have the _____ dog ever!

Name _____ Date _____

▶Homophones

▶Write a pair of homophones for each pair of definitions.

1. in this place
   listen   _____

2. two together
   a green fruit   _____

3. a tangle
   in no way   _____

4. mountain top
   a sneaky look   _____

5. a brief stop
   animal feet   _____

6. happen in history
   went by   _____

▶Use the correct homophone from above to
complete each sentence.

7. The dog's dirty _____ tracked in mud.

8. We picked a ripe _____ off the tree.

9. They need to turn up the sound so we can _____ the movie.

10. Take a quick _____ at the new kittens.

VOCABULARY

UNIT 6 Country Life • **Lesson 3** *Leah's Pony*

GRAMMAR

▶ # Review of Unit I

▶ Give the name and define the four kinds of sentences, including the correct end punctuation.

1. _____

_____

2. _____

_____

3. _____

_____

4. _____

_____

▶ Substitute the correct pronoun for the underlined noun.

5. <u>Amiri and Serena</u> _____ own a farm that is 200 years old.

6. <u>The farm</u> _____ has been in Amiri's family all those years.

▶Tone of a Personal Letter

The **tone of a personal** letter is informal and friendly, as if you were having a friendly conversation. In a personal letter, you include your own thoughts and feelings. You also use words that are colorful and informal.

Think about writing a personal letter to someone. Perhaps you have a grandparent in another state. Maybe you have a pen-pal in another country.

Think about things to write in a personal letter to this person. Maybe you are taking your dog to the pet show. Perhaps you went on a field trip to a toy factory. Maybe you have a great joke to share. List five things you could write about in a personal letter.

_____

_____

On a separate sheet of paper, write a personal letter to the person you chose. Keep the tone friendly and informal.

Be sure to include a heading with your address and the date. Don't forget to write a greeting and closing. Then sign your letter.

Address an envelope and get a stamp. Now, you are ready to mail your letter.

WRITER'S CRAFT

UNIT 6 Country Life • **Lesson 4** *Cows in the Parlor*

▶Words with Latin Roots

Rhyming Strategy
Write the words from the box that rhyme with each word.

sports	tractor	select	fines

1. forts _____

2. lines _____

3. reject _____

4. factor _____

Meaning Strategy
Write a sentence using each word below.

1. export _____

2. import _____

3. refine _____

4. finished _____

5. support _____

UNIT 6 Country Life • **Lesson 4** *Cows in the Parlor*

▶Levels of Specificity

Write some words that relate to travel under the correct categories.

Travel

Land   **Air**   **Water**

Example: train   helicopter   ski boat

_____   _____   _____

_____   _____   _____

_____   _____   _____

VOCABULARY

▶Review of Unit 2

Fill in quotation marks, commas, question marks, exclamation points, and capitals as needed.

You can buy fresh honey in yakima, washington, tucson, arizona and all over the country. Who collects all the honey on the grocery store shelf Beekeepers collect the honey for us. Queen bees worker bees and drones are the three kinds of bees. They live in hives. In the hive the worker bees store honey and pollen the drone bees mate with the queen and the queen lays her eggs. Bees go through the same four growth stages as butterflies: egg larva pupa and adult. These bees will tell us about making honey.

Why do we make honey Queen Bee asked.

Worker Bee answered We make honey to feed ourselves.

UNIT 6 Country Life • **Lesson 4** *Cows in the Parlor: A Visit to a Dairy Farm*

▶ Structure of a Business Letter

When a business letter follows a good structure, it makes a good impression and is more likely to get positive results. There are six parts to a good business letter: **heading, inside address, greeting, body, closing,** and **signature.**

Suppose that your teacher had just read two of Cynthia Rylant's books, *The Blue Hill Meadows* and *The Relatives Came* to your class. Imagine that many of your classmates have read the *Henry and Mudge* books. You think that Cynthia Rylant would make a great guest author for your school library program.

On the lines below, write a business letter using the information given, plus your own name and address. Be sure to use all six parts of a business letter. Remember to punctuate all the parts correctly.

Letter recipient: Ms. Cynthia Rylant, author of over 60 books for children

Address: Ms. Cynthia Rylant
C/O Harcourt Brace & Company
525 B Street
San Diego, California 92101

_____

_____

_____

_____

_____

WRITER'S CRAFT

UNIT 6   Country Life • **Lesson 5** *Just Plain Fancy*

▶Classify and Categorize

Amish Country Puzzler
Have the students read the words below. Ask students
to divide the words into two categories and to write
the words in the puzzle. Each group of words in the
puzzle should be from the same category. Each word
must fit in the spaces.

farmers	crafts	children	helpers	nests
farm	visitors	neighbors	organdy	chickens

__ __ __ p __ __ __

__ __ __ l __ __ __ __

__ __ a __ __ __ __ __ __

__ __ i __ __ __ __ __ __

__ n __ __ __ __ __ __ __

f __ __ __

__ __ a __ __ __

n __ __ __ __

c __ __ __ __ __ __ __

__ __ __ __ __ __ y

UNIT 6 Country Life • **Lesson 5** *Just Plain Fancy*

▶ Words with Greek Roots

Meaning Word Strategy
Fill in each blank with a word from the box that best completes each sentence.

unicycle	headphone	criticize	telephone	century

1. We are now in the 21st _____.

2. It is not nice to _____ other people.

3. My _____ has one wheel.

4. Is the _____ ringing?

5. I wear a _____ when I listen to the radio.

Foreign Language Strategy
Write the words from the box that have these roots in them.

critical	unicycle	earphone	criticize	century		
telephone	tricycle	headphone	bicycle	center	central

1. phone _____

2. critic _____

3. cent _____

4. cycle _____

SPELLING

▶Base Word Families

▶**Write the base word for each pair below.**

1. starved, starving _____

2. dreamlike, dreamy _____

3. circling, circular _____

4. spent, spending _____

5. enclose, closed _____

▶**Write four sets of word families below.**

1. _____

2. _____

3. _____

4. _____

VOCABULARY

Name _____ Date _____

▶Review of Unit 3

▶**For each pair, circle the contraction.**

1. Your/you're

2. They're/there

3. His/he's

▶**To which senses do these adjectives apply?**

4. Soft _____

5. Loud _____

6. Fuzzy _____

▶**Some words that begin with *h* take it as the indefinite article, and some words that begin with *u* take *a*. Read these phrases and circle the correct indefinite article.**

7. a/an hot day

8. a/an honest person

9. a/an union member

▶**Fill in the verb with the correct tense.**

10. Square dancing _____ from the country. (come, past)

11. Each pair _____ on one side of an imaginary square. (stand, present)

12. The dancers _____ to that position at the end of the dance. (return, future)

USAGE

UNIT 6 Country Life • **Lesson 5** *Just Plain Fancy*

▶ Collecting and Organizing Data

Writers **collect and organize data in learning logs** to help them remember observations they have made, to record changes over a period of time, and to give them ideas for writing.

Choose one of the following situations. Now, imagine that you are making regular observations and recording changes in a learning log. Think of five different times and observations. Then, use the lines below to write out your learning log entries. Remember to include the dates and times of your entries. Be sure to give your learning log a title.

You watch animals on the African plains during the day.

Over several days you observe the changes in the weather as a hurricane comes and goes.

You record the changes of activities your little sister does in her first five years of life.

_____

_____

_____

_____

_____

_____

_____

UNIT 6 Country Life • **Lesson 6** *What Ever Happened to the Baxter Place?*

▶ Main Idea and Supporting Details

Write a paragraph about a robot. Before you begin, think about these questions. What is a robot? How does the robot work? What would you want the robot to do? Would you like to have a robot of your own?

Take some notes using an encyclopedia, the Internet, or a book from the library to find out about robots. Then, write a paragraph. State the main idea of your paragraph in the first sentence. Then, use your notes to write detail sentences. Remember, every detail sentence should tell something about the main idea.

_____

_____

_____

_____

_____

_____

_____

_____

_____

_____

COMPREHENSION

▶ Words with Foreign Origins

SPELLING

Visualization Strategy
Circle the correct spelling for each word. Then write it on the line.

1. alfafa   afalfa   alfalfa   _____

2. boutiqu   boutique   boutiek   _____

3. collage   collaje   colage   _____

4. prezel   pretzal   pretzel   _____

5. armadello   armadillo   armodello   _____

6. mortgage   morgage   mortgege   _____

Meaning Strategy
Write a sentence using each word below.

1. plaza _____

2. alto _____

3. bouquet _____

4. yodel _____

5. tempo _____

Words with Foreign Origins • Challenge

Name _____ Date _____

▶Word Concept

Circle the words in each sentence that tell about the concept of each underlined word.

1. The farmer plowed lines in the dry land and filled them with water to <u>irrigate</u> the soil.

2. A cactus lives in the desert, its natural <u>habitat</u>.

3. <u>Precipitation</u> comes in the form of rain or snow.

4. Some shots make us <u>immune</u> to disease so we don't get sick.

5. The rock's <u>inertia</u> kept it from moving .

6. We studied animals in <u>zoology</u> class.

VOCABULARY

Name _____ Date _____

▶Review of Unit 4

GRAMMAR

▶**Write an X over unnecessary apostrophes.**

1. That boat is their's.

2. Everyone's pets are special to them.

▶**Underline the complete subject or subjects in these sentences, and add periods.**

3. The ten-acre orchard along Comstock Rd is owned by Ms Harvey.

4. H L Mencken, from Baltimore, and P J O'Rourke are American humor writers.

▶**Underline the predicates in these sentences.**

5. Our crop is getting bigger every year.

6. How will we have the time to pick it all?

▶**Fill in the appropriate preposition.**

7. Luther and I are going _____ Ms. Harvey's to pick apples.

8. We stand _____ ladders to get to the high branches.

▶**Circle the verb that agrees.**

9. Ms. Harvey and her pickers are/is hard workers.

10. Esperanza and Ms. Harvey has/have calluses from the hard work.

11. Ms. Harvey or Esperanza was/were the first one up today.

▶ Avoiding Wordiness

WRITER'S CRAFT

Wordiness makes writing difficult to read and understand. Readers may lose interest when writing is too wordy.

Read the paragraph below. Then rewrite the paragraph to avoid wordiness.

The very first ever television picture transmitted was transmitted in the year of 1926 by an inventor from Scotland named John Logie Baird. As part of his equipment to transmit, Baird used some very ordinary things you could find around the house, including knitting needles, an old box, a bicycle light, and a cake pan. The very first television picture transmitted was the out of focus, blurred face of a boy. Baird gave the first public demonstration in front of lots of people where he showed how television worked, later on in that very same year.

_____

_____

_____

_____

_____

_____

_____

UNIT 6 Country Life • **Lesson 7** *If you're not from the prairie*

▶Making Inferences

▶**Each sentence suggests a place. Read each sentence. On the line write the letter of the place that the sentence suggests.**

a. hospital   **b.** theater   **c.** football game

d. barnyard   **e.** art museum   **f.** store

_____ **1.** A rooster crowed at sunrise.

_____ **2.** Dr. Sneed is with a patient in room 212.

_____ **3.** The curtain rose, and the performance began.

_____ **4.** Victoria cheered when her team scored a touchdown.

_____ **5.** Jared enjoyed looking at the paintings by Picasso.

_____ **6.** Ms. Lopez paid for her milk and bread.

▶**Choose one of the places above and write a paragraph describing it, using inferences rather than naming the place specifically. Ask a partner to read your paragraph and determine which place it is.**

_____

_____

_____

_____

_____

_____

COMPREHENSION

UNIT 6   Country Life • **Lesson 7** *If you're not from the prairie*

▶Unit 6 Review

Rhyming Word Strategy Write a word from the box that rhymes with each word below.

trout	knives	flurry

1. hurry _____

2. scout _____

3. wives _____

Visualization Strategy Write the correct spelling for each word. Then use each word in a sentence of your own.

1. travelars _____

_____

2. dirtyest _____

_____

3. cicling _____

_____

4. messeges _____

_____

5. sillyer _____

_____

SPELLING

UNIT 6 Country Life • **Lesson 7** *If you're not from the prairie*

▶Unit 6 Review

Write whether each pair of words are synonyms, antonyms, homophones, or family words.

1. rows, rose _____

2. riches, wealth _____

3. comical, comedy _____

4. push, pull _____

5. sum, some _____

6. show, hide _____

7. history, historic _____

8. winner, champion _____

UNIT 6 Country Life • **Lesson 7** *If you're not from the prairie*

▶Review of Unit 5

▶ **Fill in the blanks and add needed colons and commas in this paragraph about the grammar, usage, and mechanics skills in this lesson. Use your Handbook if you wish.**

A simple sentence _____

Simple sentences can be joined to make _____

sentences. Three conjunctions most commonly connect simple

sentences into compound sentences *and but* and *or.* Conjunctions are

words that _____.

▶ **Answer *T* for true or *F* for false.**

1. Book titles should be underlined or italicized.

_____

2. Movie titles should not be underlined or italicized.

_____

3. The titles of short poems should be underlined or italicized.

_____

4. The names of the days of the week should be capitalized.

_____

5. All words in a book title should be capitalized.

_____

MECHANICS

UNIT 6   Country Life • **Lesson 7** *If you're not from the prairie*

▶Graphic Organizers

WRITER'S CRAFT

Graphic organizers are simple drawings that help writers remember and organize their ideas for writing. Graphic organizers help writers get started by providing a plan to follow.

Think of the activities and things that have happened to you in the past week. Use the Chain of Events Graphic Organizer below to record the events of your week.

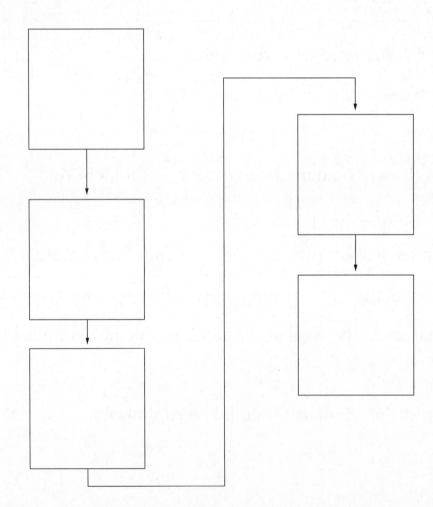

Graphic Organizers • **Challenge**